SIMPLE LESSONS • FUN PRACTICE ~~PAGES~~ • EASY EXAMPLES

BASICS FOR KIDS

AND BEGINNERS

BY COACH JOHN

Copyright © 2014 Coach John

All rights reserved.

Author: Coach John

Contributing Author and Photo Credit: Mrs. Coach John

ACKNOWLEDGEMENTS

Thank you to my **WIFE** who supported me in trying something new, and who helped me with the finer points of this book. If it was not for her contributions and encouragement, this book might only be half-complete.

Thank you to my **CHILDREN** who enthusiastically wanted to learn about hockey and who asked magnificent questions. This is a skill that will serve them well during their hockey career and any future endeavor they choose.

In addition, a special thank you to my **CHILDREN** for their dedication in reading this book and completing the practice pages many times over. They gave me their honest feedback about how kids think and how they like the pages to look. Their enthusiasm to complete the same work over and over again energized me to continue on.

I would like to thank my **FRIENDS** who helped me review the book from a professional perspective, and for their questions and ideas.

To the **HOCKEY PARENTS**, who give their time, energy, and money to the sport. They rush to make it on time. They carry heavy bags though slushy parking lots. They spend countless hours standing in cold arenas gripping a lukewarm cup of coffee. They tie skates, snap straps, and squeeze on shirts. They cheer every effort, no matter how big or small, by their child or another. They smile while a group of 10 wobbly-legged children skate themselves into a corner of the rink. The children slip, fall, and knock into each other, in a chase to only touch the puck, whack it towards the net, and watch it bewilderingly slide between the goalie's legs.

To the parents who encourage their kids to learn a new and challenging skill, I sincerely thank you. **Hockey parents are among the best parents in the world.**

See you at the Barn!

Hockey Basics for Kids and Beginners

By: Coach John

THE LAYOUT OF THE ICE 1

    The Ice Rink 2
    The Benches 2
        Practice: Help the Players 3
    The Lines 4
        Practice: Color the Lines 5
        Practice: Find the Lines 5
    The Circles and Dots 6
        Practice: Circles and Dots 7
    The Nets 8
        Practice: Missing Pieces 10
        Practice: The Layout of the Ice - Word Find 11
        Practice: Draw an Ice Hockey Rink 12

THE PEOPLE 13

    Players 13
    Coaches 13
    Referee 13
    Timekeeper 13
        Fun Page 14

THE EQUIPMENT 15

    Protective Equipment 15
    Learn How to Dress 16
    Skate Sharpening 17
        Practice: Dress the Player 19
    Team Shirts 20
    Pucks 20
    Sticks 21
        Practice: Connect the Picture to the Word 23
        Practice: Protective Equipment Crossword 24

THE PLAYERS AND POSITIONS 25

- THE GOALIE 26
- THE DEFENSE 27
- THE FORWARDS 29
- PLAYING YOUR POSITION 31
  - Practice: Forwards and Positions 32
  - Practice: Who is not in the correct position 33
  - Practice: Who is not in the correct position 34

THE GAME 35

- STARTING THE GAME 35
- STARTING A FACE-OFF 36
  - Practice: Start The Game 37
- SCORING 38
  - Practice: Break Away Maze 39
- KEEPING TIME 40
- THE SCORE BOARD 40
- TELLING THE SCORE 41
- VERSUS 41
- WINNING 42
  - Practice: Word Find with Mystery Code 43
- ZONES 44
  - Practice: Know the Zones 48
  - Practice: Stay in the correct zone 49
  - Fun Page 50

THE RULES 51

- ICING 51
- OFF-SIDE 52
  - Practice: You make the call 53
  - Practice: You make the call 54
- PENALTIES 55
- COMMON PENALTIES 56
- OOPS !?! 56

CONGRATULATIONS 57

- Fun Page 58

FINAL TEST AND CERTIFICATE 59

- Fun Page 64
- Answer Pages 65

INDEX OF WORDS LEARNED 69

The Layout of the Ice

Let's learn about the parts of an Ice Hockey Rink.

The hockey rink has circles, dots, and lines on it.
It also has different areas for players to sit. Let's get started.

An Ice Hockey Rink

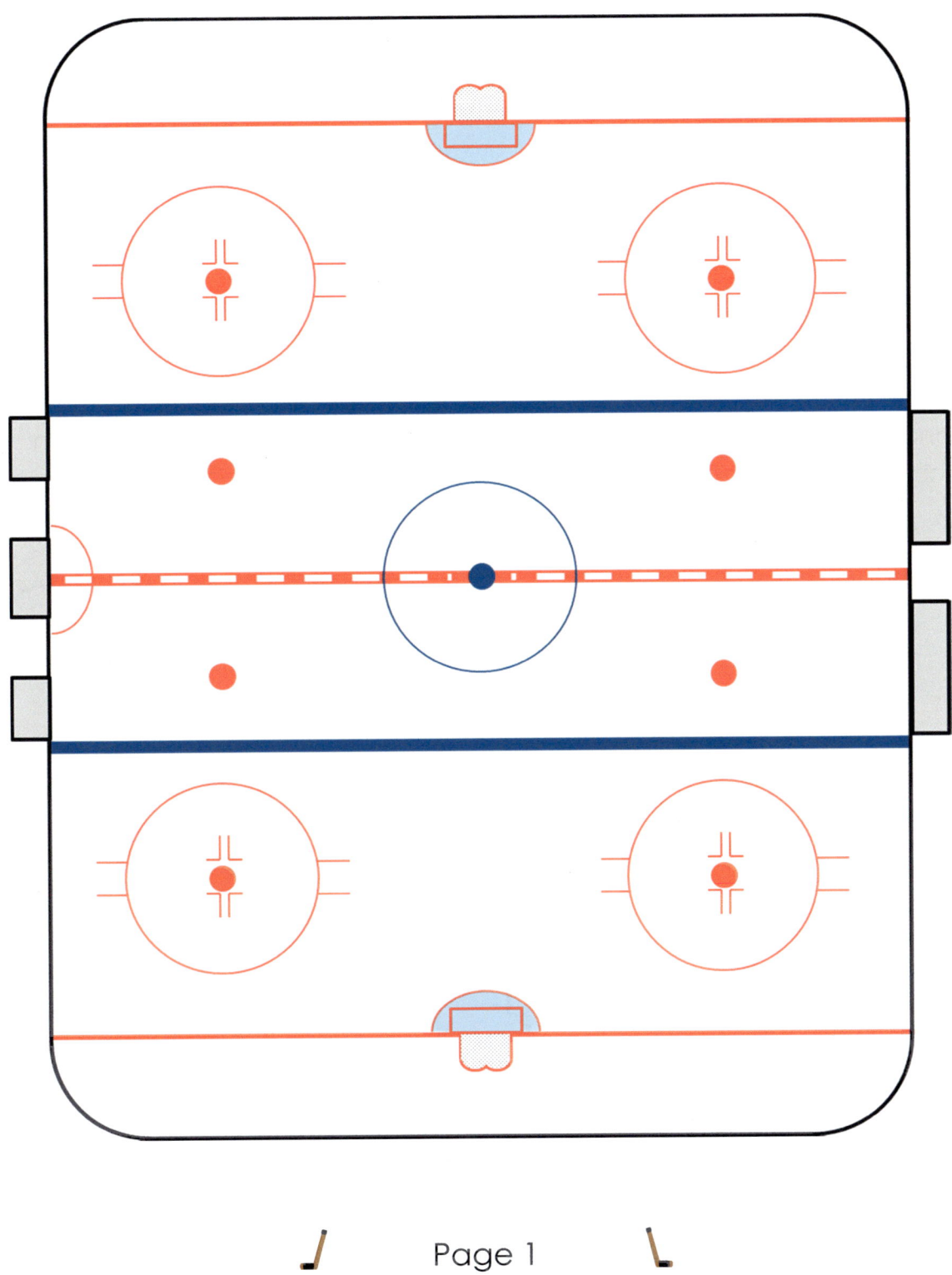

The Ice Rink

Ice hockey is played on a **SHEET** of ice called a **RINK**. The ice hockey rink is long with rounded corners.

The sheet of ice is surrounded by **BOARDS**. The boards are made of white plastic and have a yellow and red plastic trim. The boards have thick clear plastic on top of them called **GLASS**, so the hockey **FANS** can safely watch the game.

The Benches

On the side of the rink will be 2 long benches. One bench is where the **HOME** team sits. The other bench is where the **VISITOR** team sits.

Opposite, or sometimes next to the team benches, will be 3 sitting areas. The middle bench is for the **TIMEKEEPER**. This person runs the game clock, keeps score, and records the penalties. On each side of the Timekeeper, there will be a **PENALTY BOX**. One penalty box will be for the Home team and the other for the Visitor team. If a player breaks the rules of hockey, they might be sent to the penalty box for a time-out.

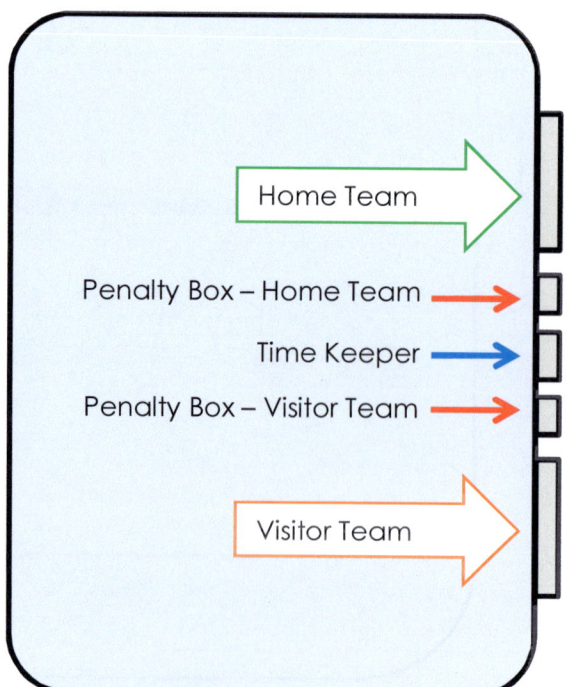

Page 2

PRACTICE: HELP THE PLAYERS

Help the players find their bench.
Draw a line to where they should sit on their team bench.
Hint: See Ice Hockey Rink #1 and Ice Hockey Rink #2 on previous page.

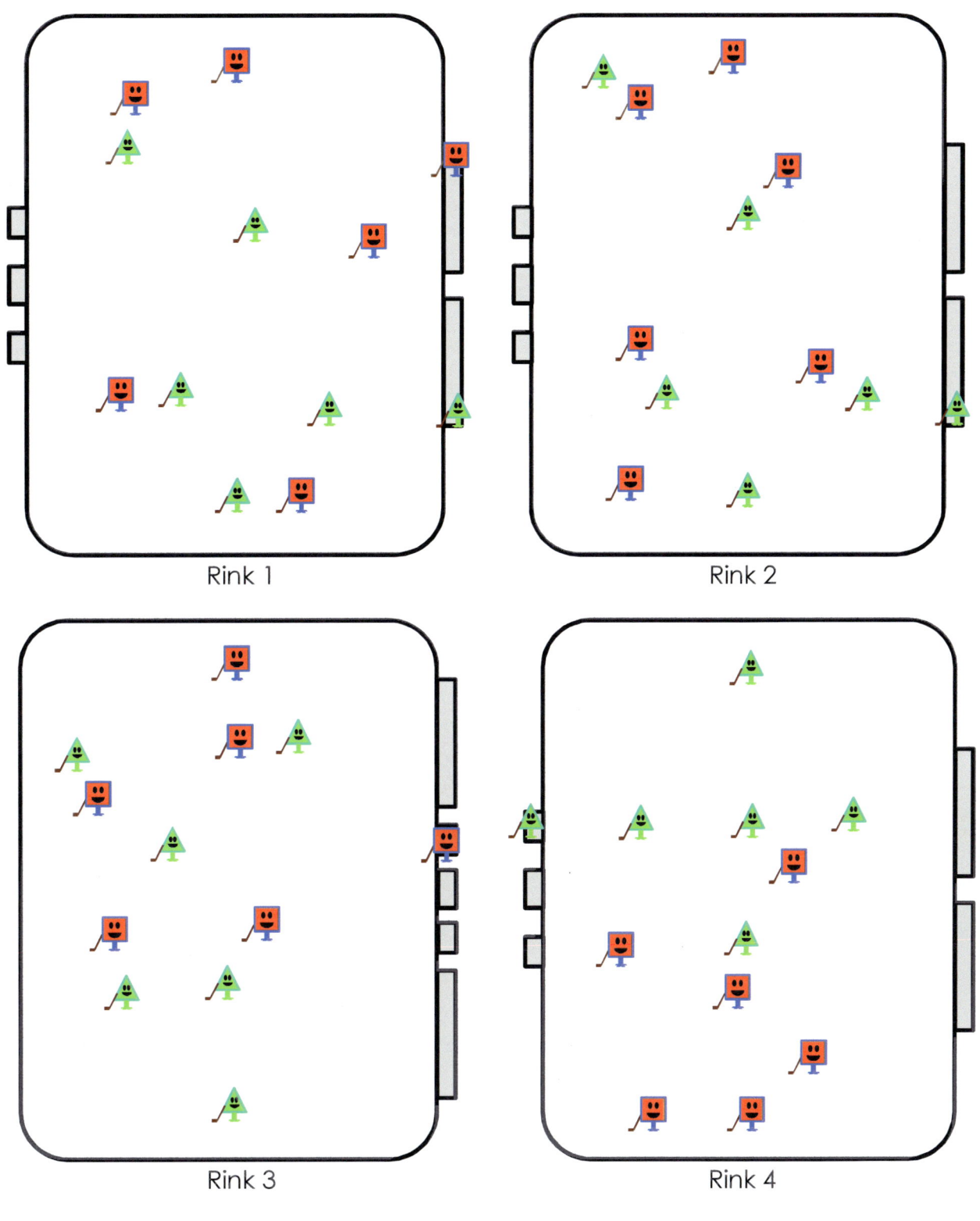

Page 3

The Lines

The hockey rink is divided in half by the **RED LINE**.
Sometimes the red line is solid ▬▬ and sometimes it is dashed. ▭▬▭

Each half of the rink has a **BLUE LINE**. ▬▬

At each end of the rink is a thin red line called the **GOAL LINE**. ―――

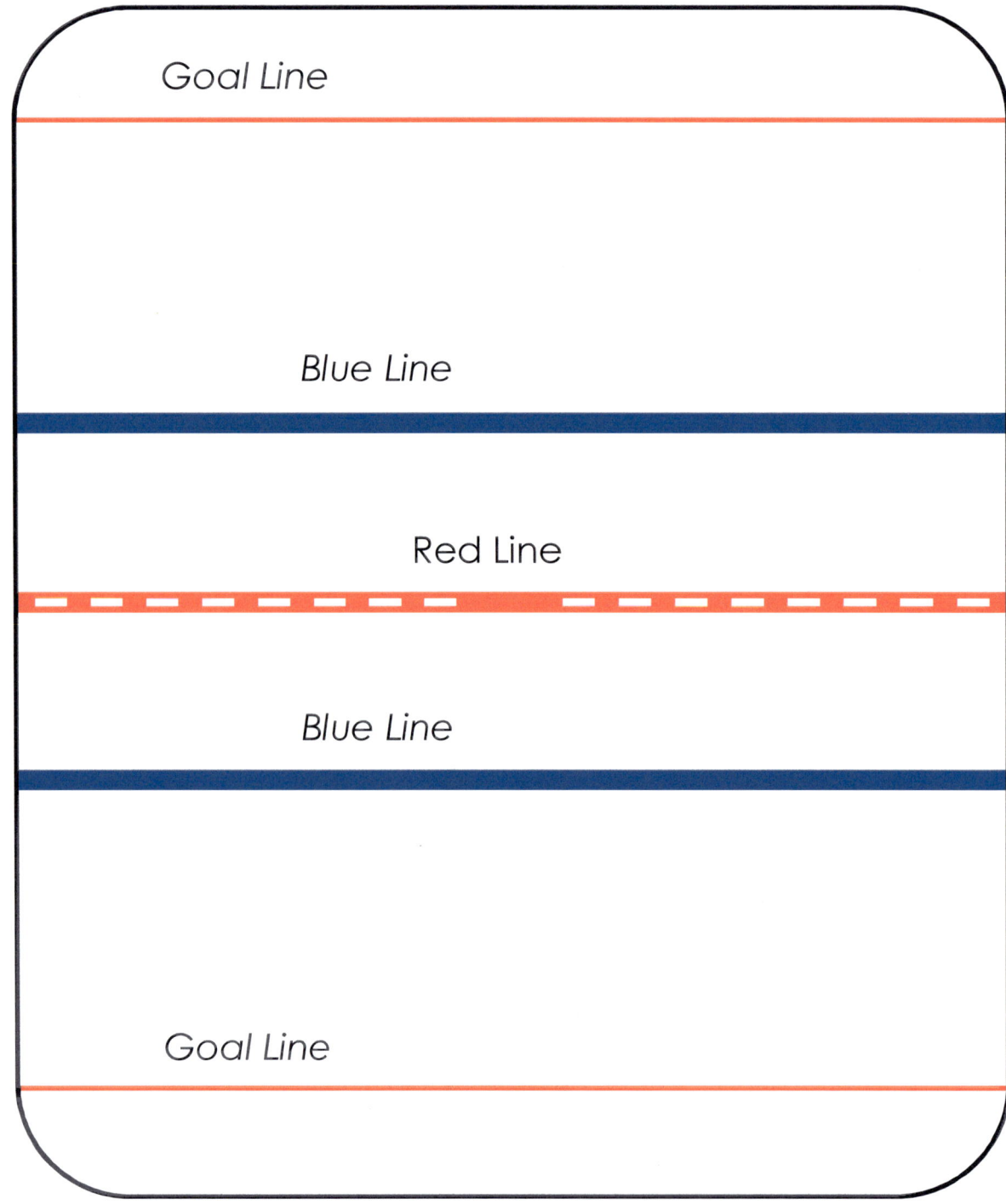

PRACTICE: COLOR THE LINES

Color the Lines of the Ice Rink

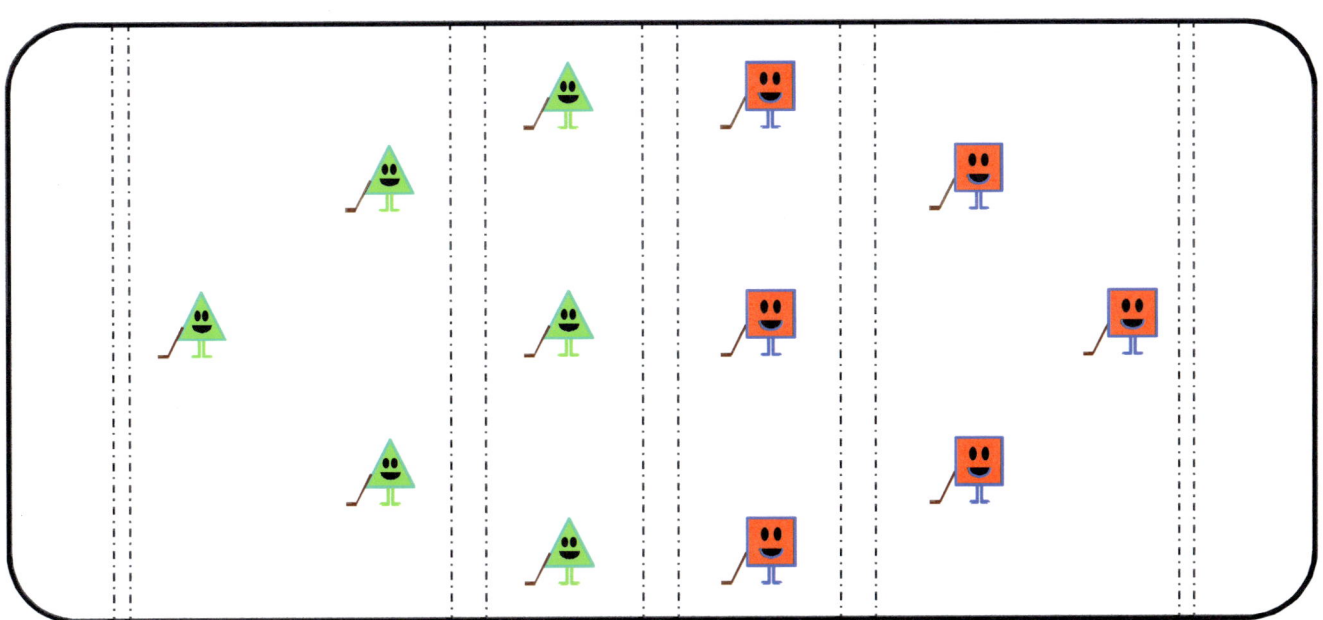

PRACTICE: FIND THE LINES

Circle the hockey rink that has the correct lines.

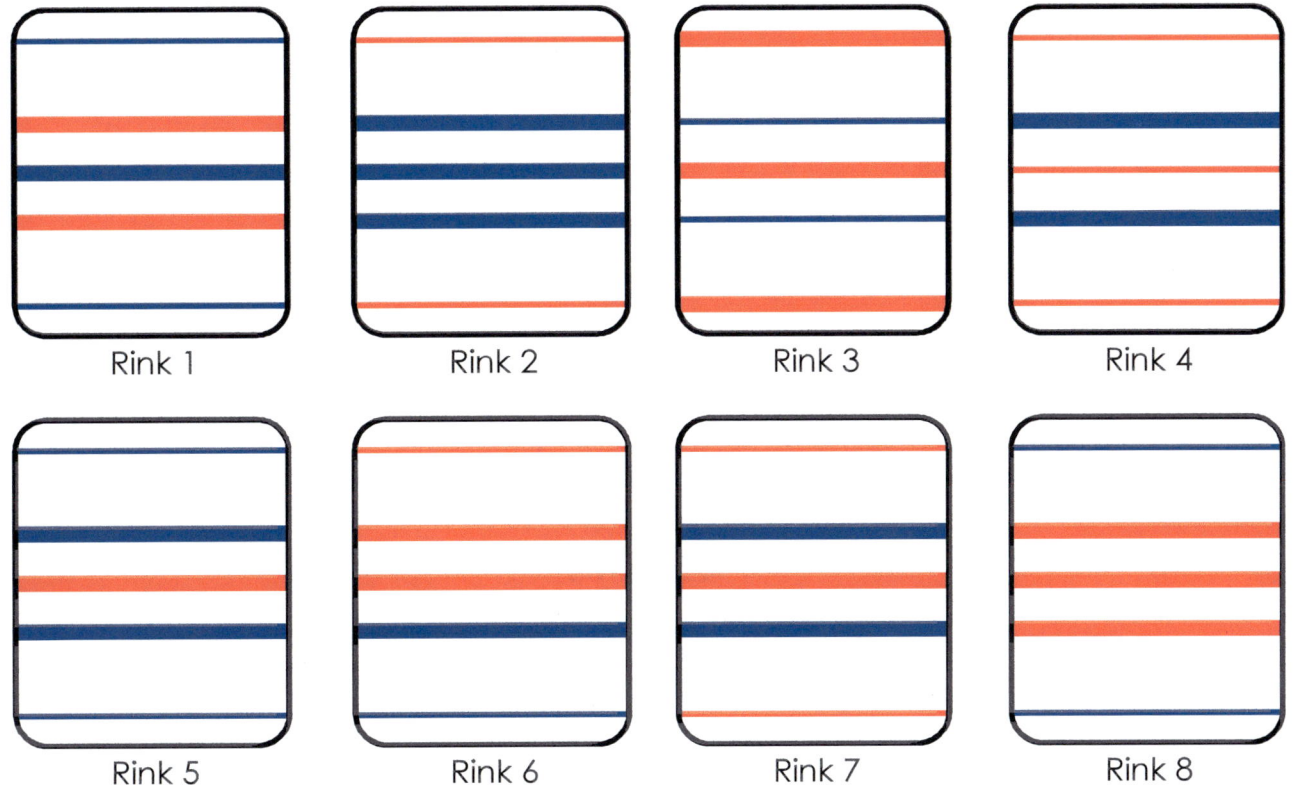

The Circles and Dots

There are many **CIRCLES** ◯ and **DOTS** ● on the ice rink. The **CIRCLES** on the ice rink help players know where to stand at different times during the game. The **DOTS** are where the puck will be dropped to start the game.

There are four red circles with red dots. The circle and dot in the middle of the ice is blue. The dot in the blue circle is called **CENTER ICE**.

The short lines on the outside of the circle are called **HASH MARKS**.

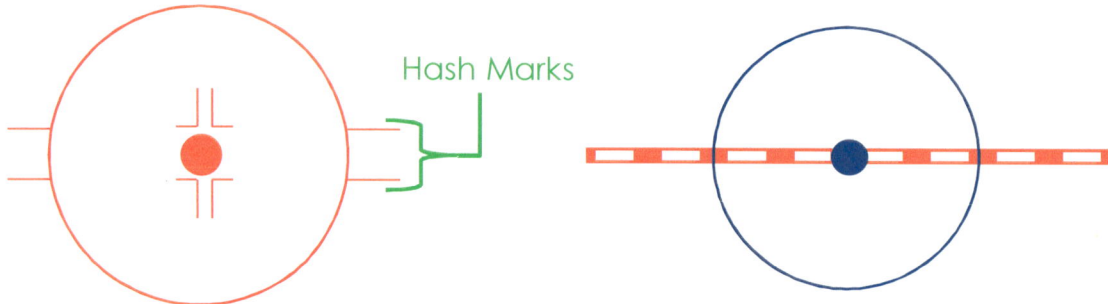

A circle with a dot in the middle.   **The Center Ice circle and dot.**

A **FACE-OFF** happens when two teams are on their side of the circle, waiting to start the game. It is called a face-off because each player faces a player from the other team.

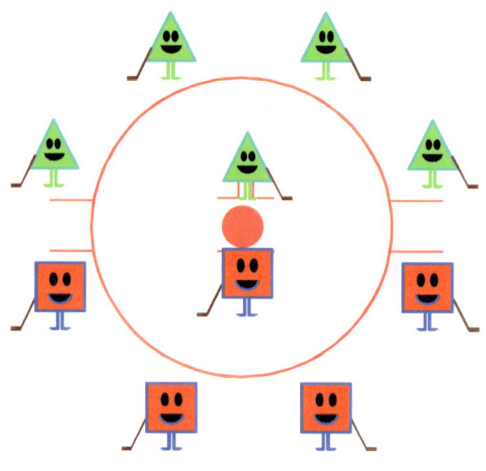

A face-off

There is a special half circle called the **REFEREE CREASE** or Referee half-circle. It is a private area where only the Referee can enter to talk to the Timekeeper, when the game is stopped. When the games is in play, it is ok to skate through the Referee Crease.

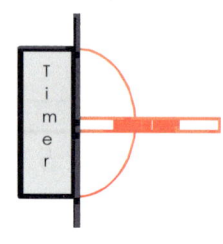

Practice: Circles and Dots

Draw the CIRCLES and color the DOTS

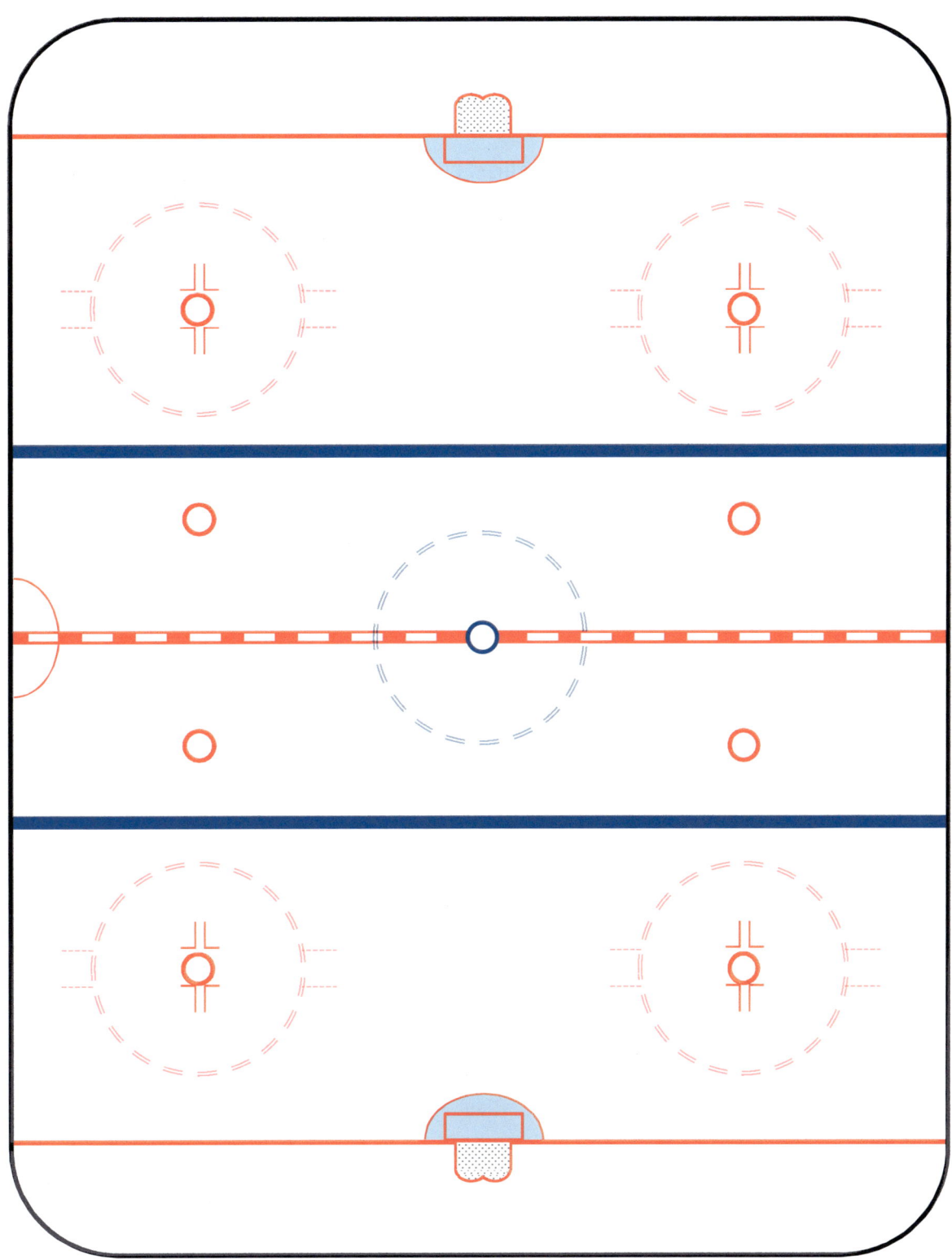

The Nets

At each end of the ice rink are the **NETS**. Each team tries to put the puck into the other team's net.

The net has two upright bars; each called a **POST** or **GOAL POST**.

The bar connecting the two posts is called a **CROSSBAR**.

At the back of the net is a white mesh called the **NET** or **NETTING**.

On the ice, in front of the net is a half circle with blue ice. In the half circle is a rectangle. This whole area is called the **CREASE**.

Front View of a Net   **Top View of a Net**

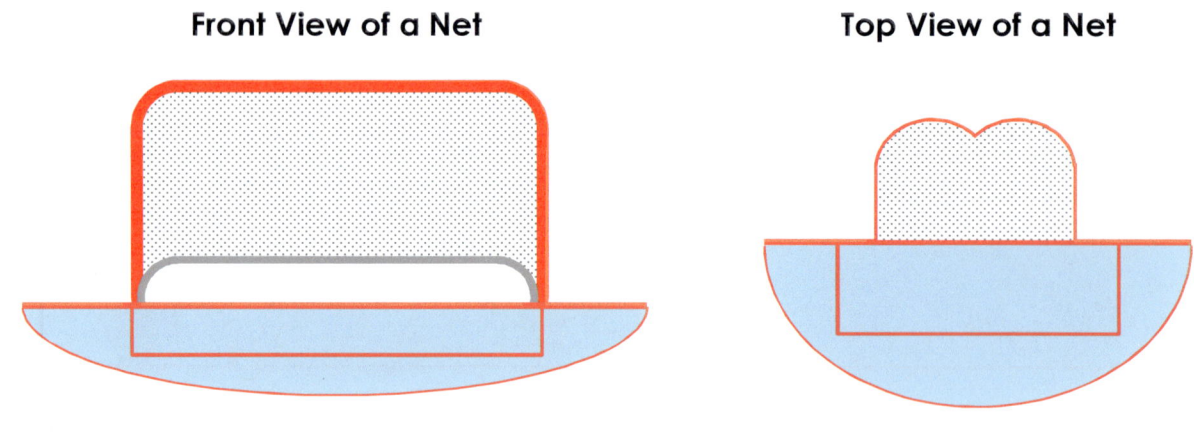

Now you know the pieces of an Ice Hockey Rink

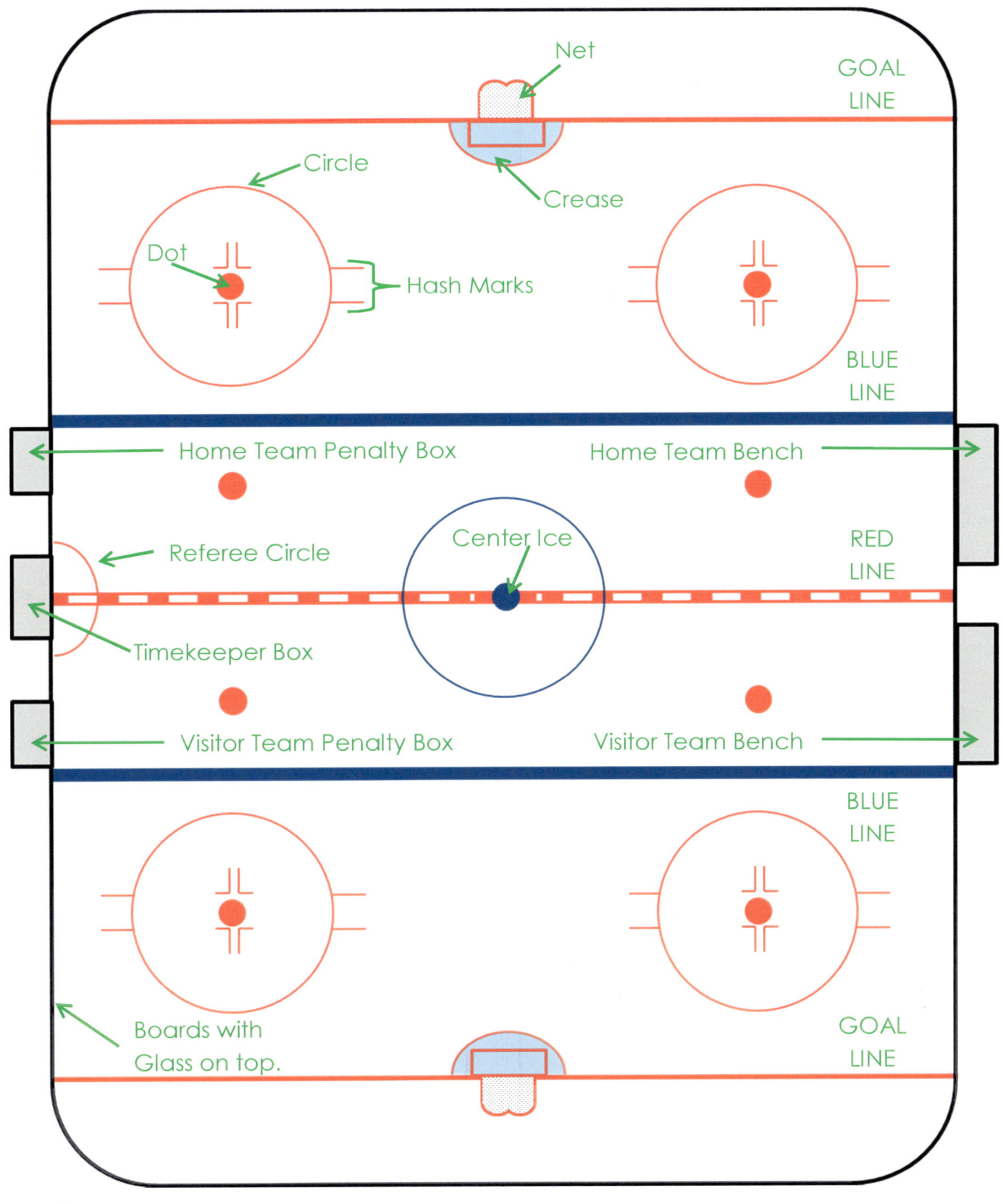

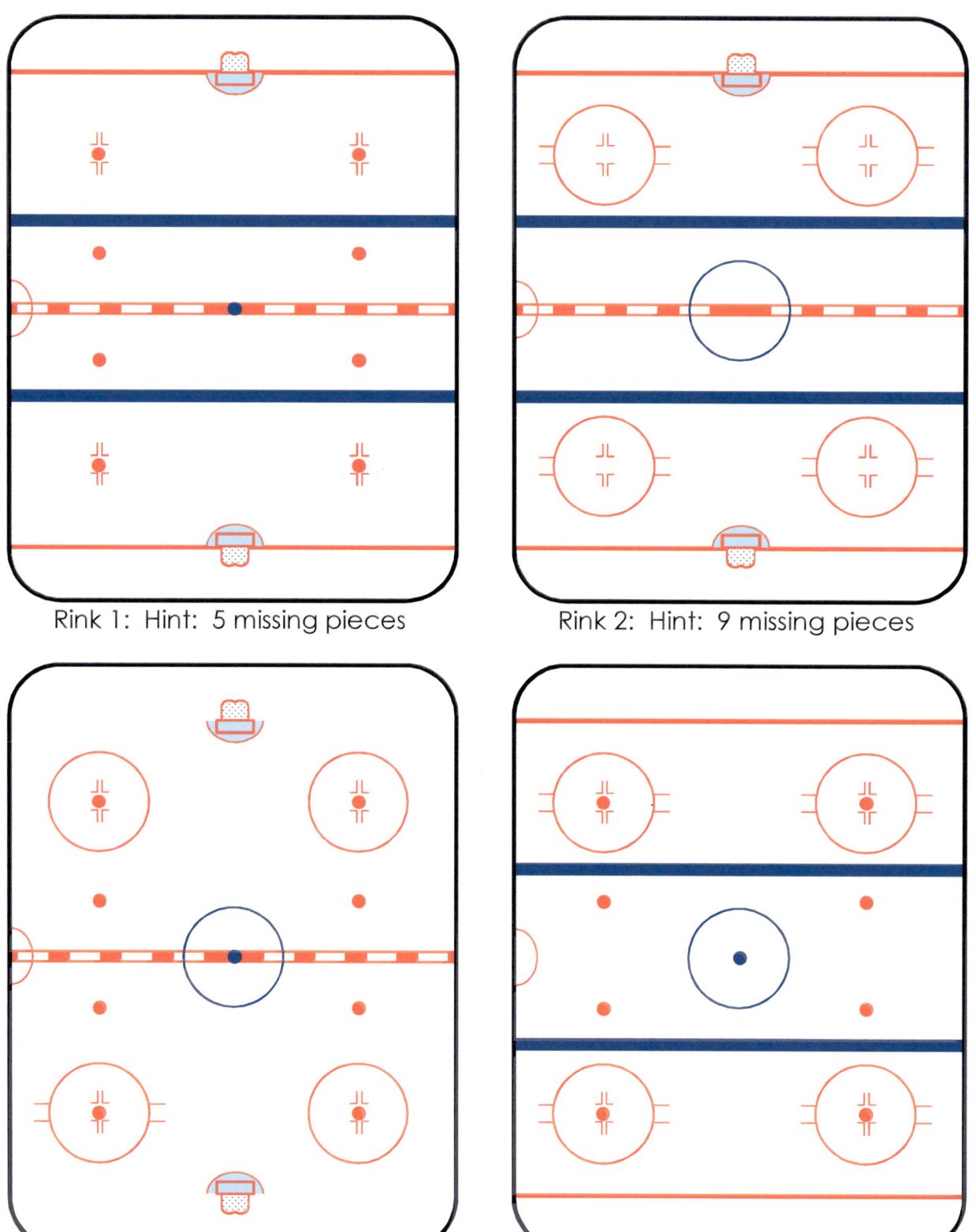

Practice: The Layout of the Ice - Word Find

Find the Words you learned about in The Layout of the Ice

P	Y	R	V	U	U	D	F	C	G	R	B	L	U	E	L	I	N	E	S
D	E	Q	E	E	M	F	A	R	L	E	L	T	T	D	C	C	H	D	C
S	O	N	X	D	O	O	N	E	A	P	Y	E	A	P	L	H	F	R	O
F	K	O	A	E	L	I	Y	A	S	E	N	X	O	S	H	E	E	T	R
A	H	R	C	L	P	I	W	S	S	E	I	L	Z	Q	S	K	A	V	E
N	I	A	A	J	T	A	N	E	I	K	R	T	P	Q	T	X	M	F	J
S	F	G	E	M	H	Y	G	E	R	E	C	R	I	N	K	V	R	E	A
G	U	C	G	Y	H	W	B	Q	Q	M	R	V	Z	F	I	M	D	X	S
P	O	J	G	W	I	S	K	O	Q	I	O	S	I	N	K	O	P	E	I
O	C	A	Z	A	N	I	A	C	X	T	S	E	S	S	T	S	L	A	S
S	F	W	L	E	Y	P	I	H	J	B	S	H	N	S	I	C	Y	D	O
T	R	K	M	L	K	F	Y	Z	L	W	B	C	X	Q	R	T	R	C	H
U	Y	O	S	G	I	U	O	G	O	A	A	N	L	I	A	A	O	J	T
E	H	G	N	U	Q	N	K	P	F	W	R	E	C	L	O	P	I	R	H
F	N	X	X	Q	Q	O	E	E	M	K	M	B	T	B	V	M	M	R	P

BENCHES	CROSSBAR	GOALLINE	PENALTYBOX	SCORE
BLUELINE	DOTS	HASHMARKS	POST	SHEET
BOARDS	FACEOFF	HOME	REDLINE	TIMEKEEPER
CIRCLES	FANS	NET	RINK	VISITOR
CREASE	GLASS			

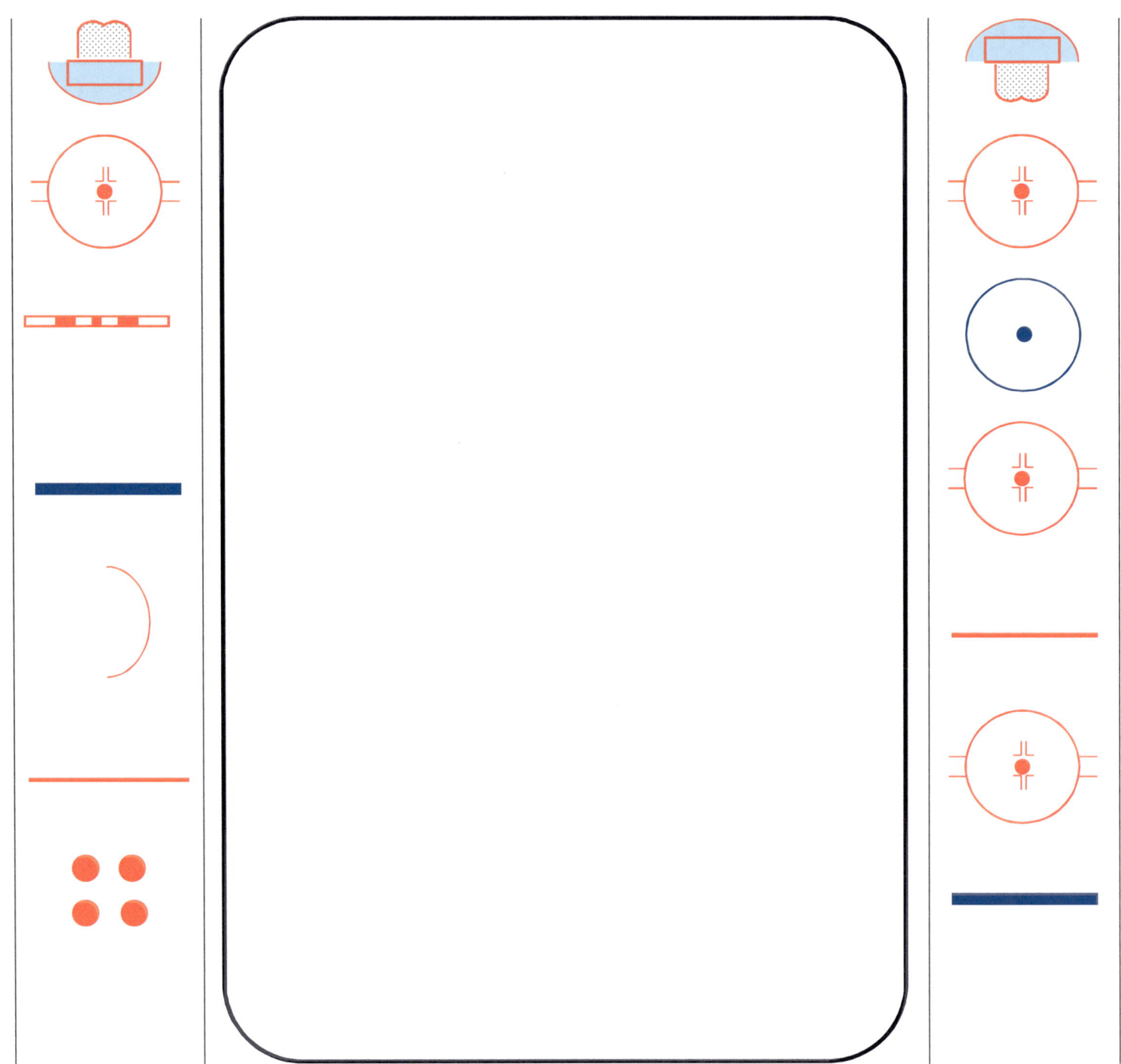

THE PEOPLE

Players

The Players are the people who play the game. All the hockey players together make up the hockey **TEAM**. Each player has a place or **POSITION** on the ice. There are different **POSITIONS** for different players. There are **FORWARD PLAYERS**, **DEFENSE PLAYERS**, and **GOALIES**.

Coaches

A team of hockey players will have one or more leaders called a **COACH**. The Coaches are the teachers and leaders of the team. There will be a **HEAD COACH** who is in charge. The Head Coach might have helper Coaches who are called **ASSISTANT COACHES**. Your Coaches are there to help you. If you have a question or need help, you can ask any of your coaches. During a hockey practice, your coach will blow a **WHISTLE** when it is time to start or stop.

Referee

The job of the **REFEREE** is to keep the game fair. There may be 1, 2, 3 or 4 Referees on the ice during a hockey game. You can easily find them because they will be wearing a black and white striped shirt. If a hockey rule is broken, they will blow their whistle very loud. When you hear their whistle, it is time to stop playing.

Timekeeper

The **TIMEKEEPER** will be a person who sits in the Timekeeper box. They will start and stop the clock during the game, and record goals and penalties. Sometimes the Referee will talk to the Timekeeper to tell who scored a goal or who is going to get a penalty. The Timekeeper uses a very loud buzzer to tell everyone that the clock has stopped.

Fun Page

Draw a picture of you playing hockey.

Send it to Coach John and we might put it on our website
www.HockeyCoachJohn.com

(Ask a parent)

The Equipment

Protective Equipment

Hockey players wear many different pieces of **EQUIPMENT** to protect them.

Learn How to Dress

Putting on all the protective equipment can be confusing. Let's go through the order of how to get dressed to play hockey.

1	All of the equipment should be stored in a hockey **BAG**. Some hockey bags have wheels.	
2	Put on the protective **CUP** and jock. Sometimes this piece of equipment looks like a pair of shorts.	
3	Optional: If the protective cup doesn't have a built in **GARTER BELT** or Velcro strips then you may need to wear a garter belt to hold up the socks.	
4	The **SHIN GUARDS** help protect your knees when you fall and your legs from pucks and sticks. Be sure to notice that they are labelled Right and Left.	
5	Hockey **SOCKS** are worn on top of the shin guards. They are thick to keep you warm. Attach the top of the hockey sock to the garter belt or the Velcro strip on your protective cup. This keeps the socks from falling down while you are skating.	
6	It's time to put on the hockey **PANTS**. The pant legs should be wide enough to easily pull over the shin guards and fit comfortably over the protective cup. Most pants come with a belt to tighten around the waist. If the pants are loose and keep falling down, you can attach suspenders to the pants. (Item 9)	
7	Now is a good time to put on the ice **SKATES**. Since you are only half dressed, it will be easier to bend down and put on your skates. Be careful because, the **SKATE BLADES** are sharp.	
8	Put on the **SHOULDER PADS**. They slip over top your head and fasten around your body and around each arm.	

9	Optional: If you have **SUSPENDERS**, pull them up over top the shoulder pads. Not only do suspenders keep your pants up, but they help to keep your shoulder pads down. Check to see if the pants have buttons for suspenders. Once attached, the suspenders stay on the pants all season. They do not need to be removed after each game.	
10	Put the **ELBOW PADS** on around your elbows. Notice that they are labeled Right (R) and Left (L).	
11	It's time to put on the hockey **SHIRT**. It should be big enough to fit over top your shoulder pads and elbow pads. The number goes on the back. It can be difficult to put on, and even big kids get help from their team mates to put it on.	
12	Put your **NECK GUARD** on around your neck. Find a neck guard that is comfortable for you to wear. It has to be tight enough to protect your neck.	
13	Pull the **HELMET** over top your head. Make sure to fasten the chin strap which goes from ear to ear under your chin. Then fasten the face mask. One strap on each side of the face mask will snap onto the helmet somewhere near or behind the ears.	
14	Put the **GLOVES** on your hands. The gloves will help keep you warm, help you grip your hockey stick, and protect you from pucks and sticks.	
15	Now get your **STICK** and you are ready to PLAY HOCKEY.	

Skate Sharpening

Ice is slippery, even when wearing ice skates. In order for the ice skates to grip the ice, they should be properly sharpened. Skate **BLADES** have edges that cut into the ice and help a skater stay upright while turning. If the edges are dull, a skater has difficulty making turns and skating fast. An ice skate sharpening center is usually located in an ice arena.

Notice that some equipment covers up other equipment.

Wear comfortable clothes, like thermal underwear, under your hockey equipment.

The equipment is like a suit of armor.

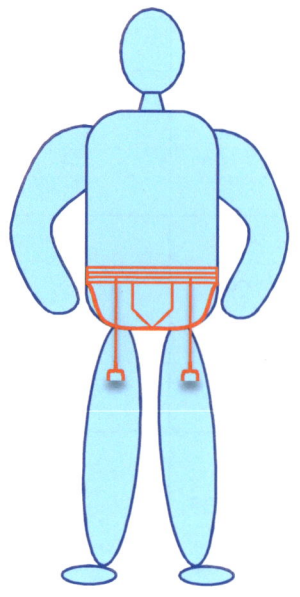
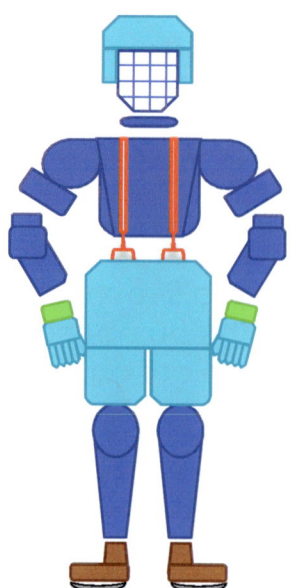

The shirt, pants, and socks cover most of the equipment.

PRACTICE: DRESS THE PLAYER

Help the Player put on the equipment.
Draw the equipment on the body where it should be worn.

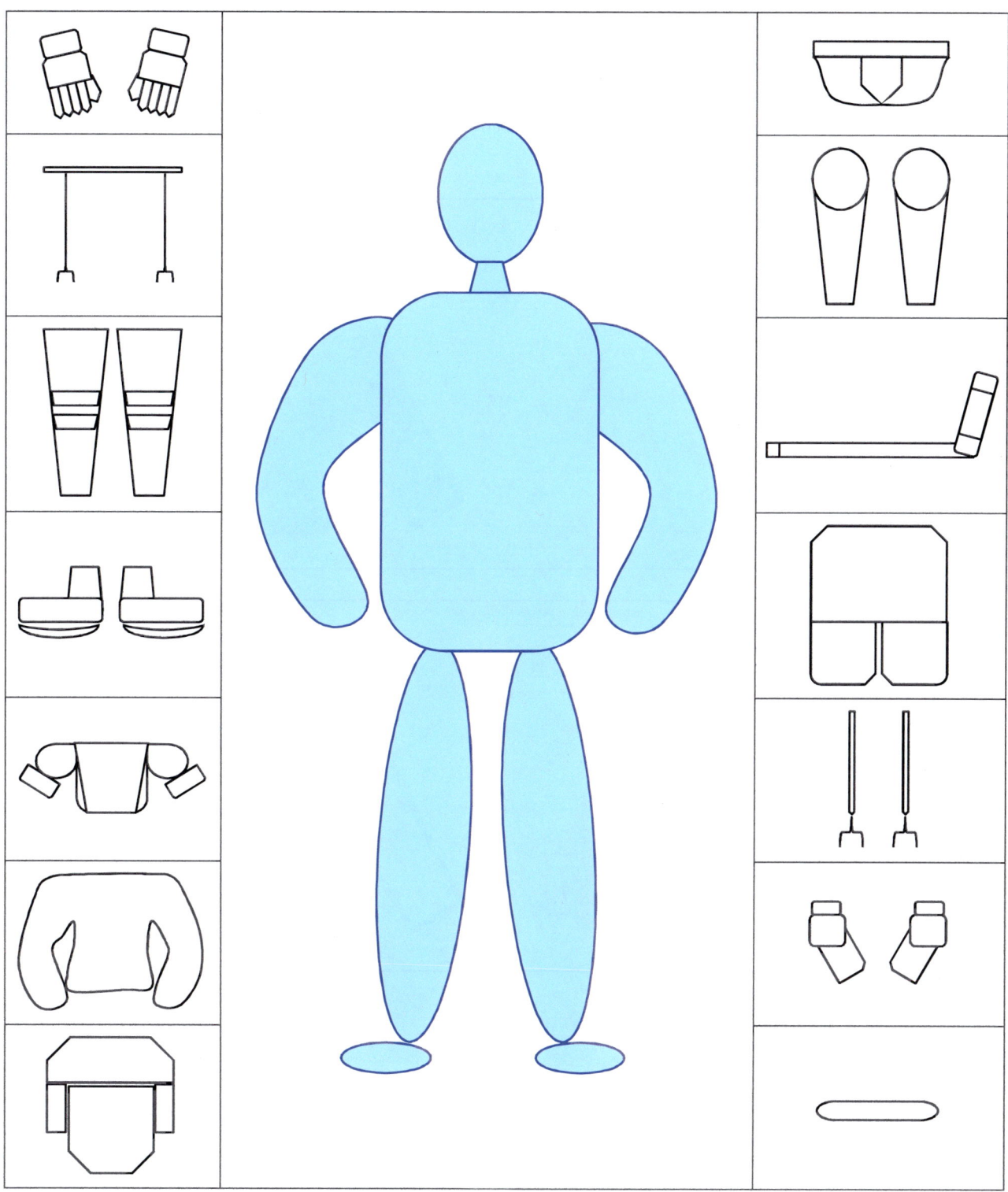

Page 19

Team Shirts

Each player will have their own *SHIRT*, sometimes called a *JERSEY* or a *SWEATER*. Usually the Home team will wear WHITE shirts and the Visitor team will wear shirts that are a COLOR. This is the tradition just in case two of the same colored teams try to play each other. On the front of the jersey is the team name or logo. On the back of the jersey will be a number and sometimes the name of the player. The numbers traditionally range from 1 to 30, with the number 1 and 30 typically reserved for the goalie.

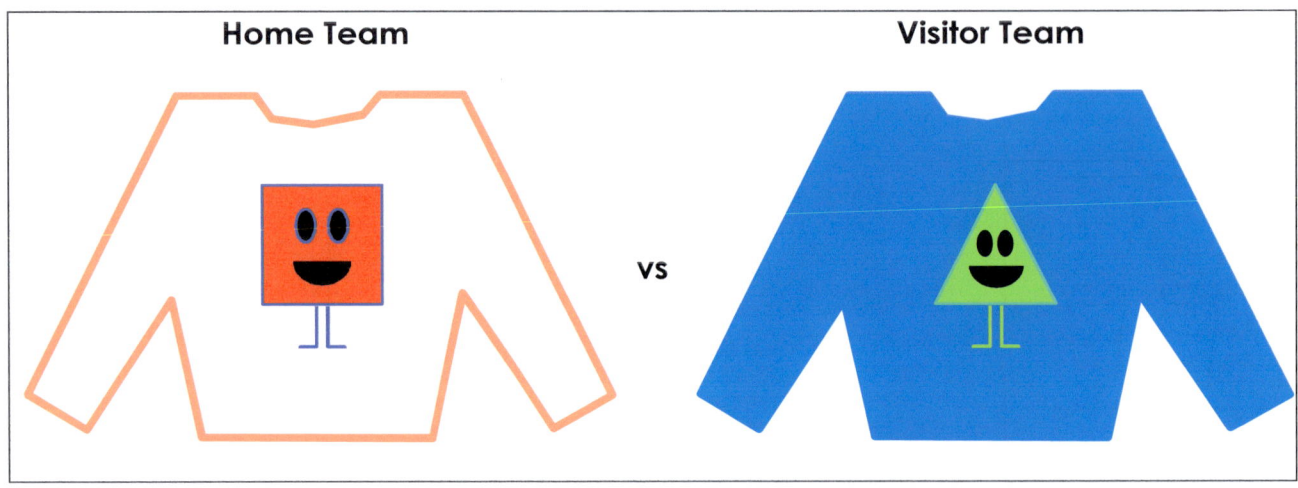

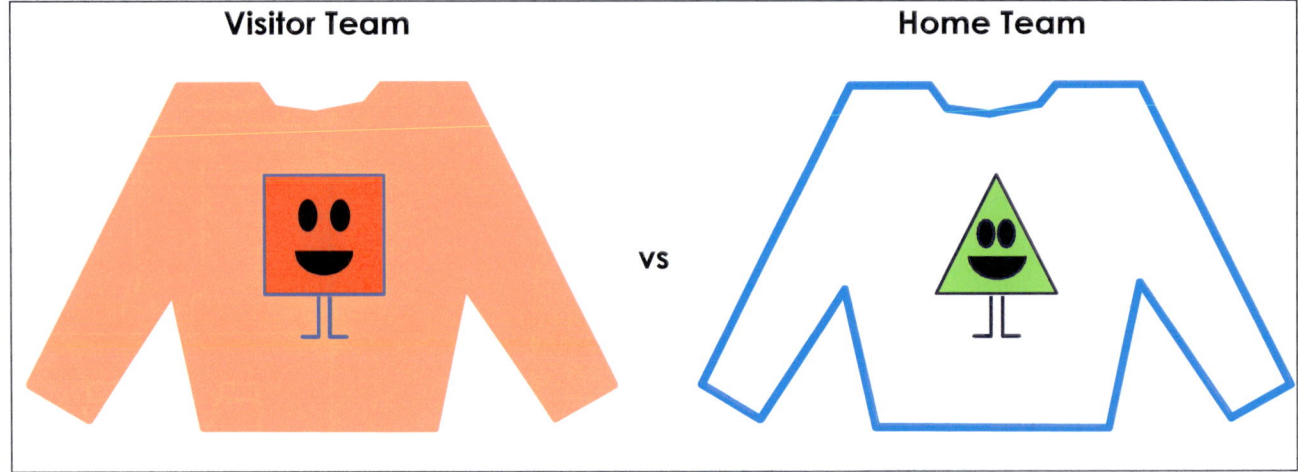

Pucks

A *PUCK* is a small hard rubber disc. Ice hockey pucks are black, blue, or green. The hockey player uses their stick to move the puck around on the ice.

Sticks

Hockey players use a **STICK** to move the puck around. A hockey player cannot use their hands to carry the puck. A goalie stick is used to stop and shoot the puck. A goalie can use their hand to cover a puck, but not to throw the puck.

A Player Stick   **A Goalie Stick**

If a hockey player likes to have the puck on the left side of their body then they would use a **LEFT HANDED** or **LH** stick. If they like the puck on their right side, then they would use a **RIGHT HANDED** or **RH** stick.

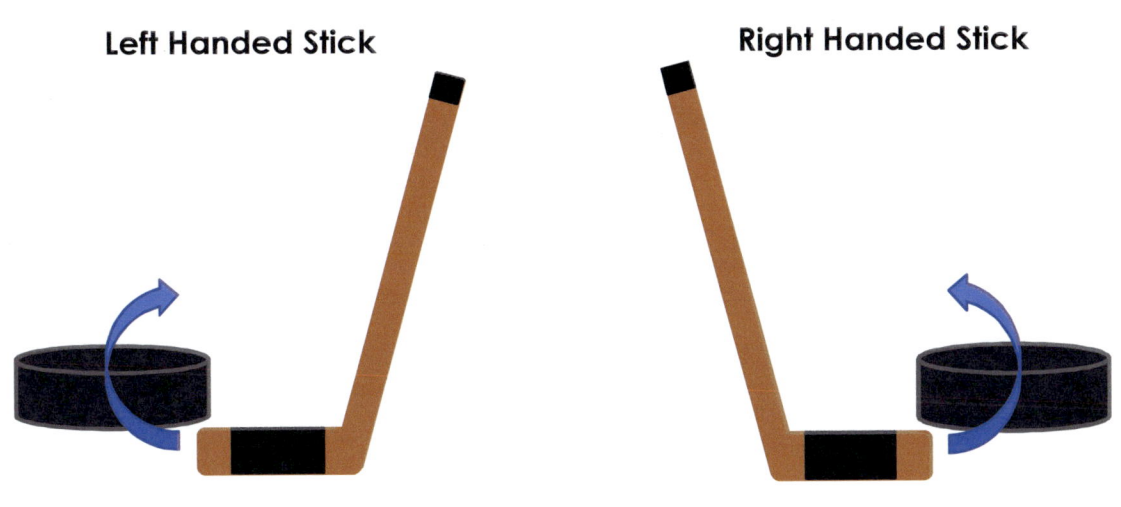

Left Handed Stick   **Right Handed Stick**

There are 3 main parts to a hockey stick.

PART 1: The top of the stick is called the **KNOB** or the **BUTT-END** of the stick. Players wrap hockey **TAPE** around this end of the stick. This helps the player to hold the stick and prevents the player's top hand from slipping off the end.

PART 2: The **SHAFT** of the stick is the long middle part of the stick. The shaft can be made of wood, fiber glass or other lightweight materials. The lighter materials help to shoot the puck harder. Most players start out using a wooden shaft. As a beginner player, when standing straight up with skates on, the shaft of the stick should be cut to just under the player's chin.

PART 3: The bottom part which slides along the ice is called a **BLADE**. Players like to wrap hockey **TAPE** around the blade to help control the puck. The blade can be straight or curved. The curve of a blade can help to shoot the puck higher. **STICK HANDLING** is when a player moves the puck from side to side using their stick.

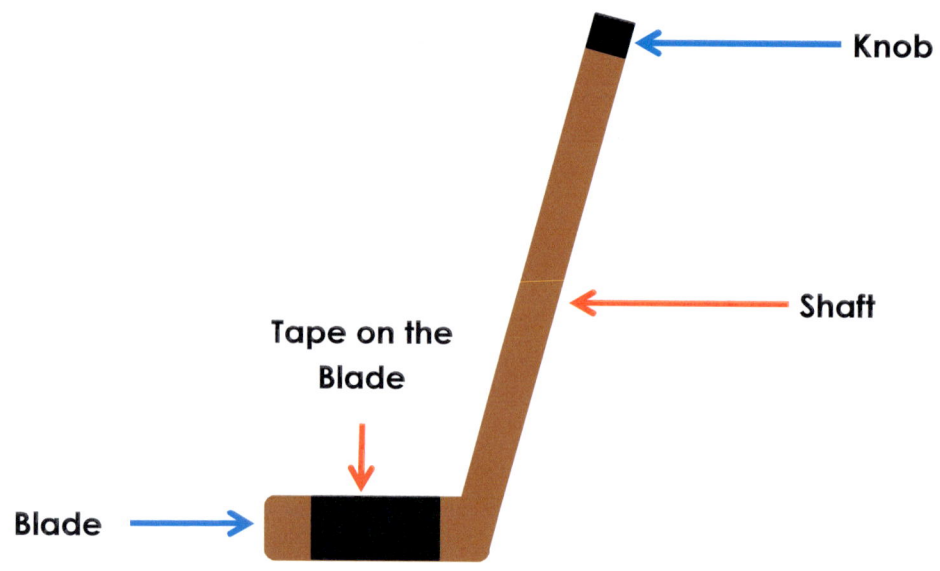

Practice: Connect the Picture to the Word

Use a Ruler to connect the dots from the picture to the correct word.
Help the players pass the puck and score a goal.

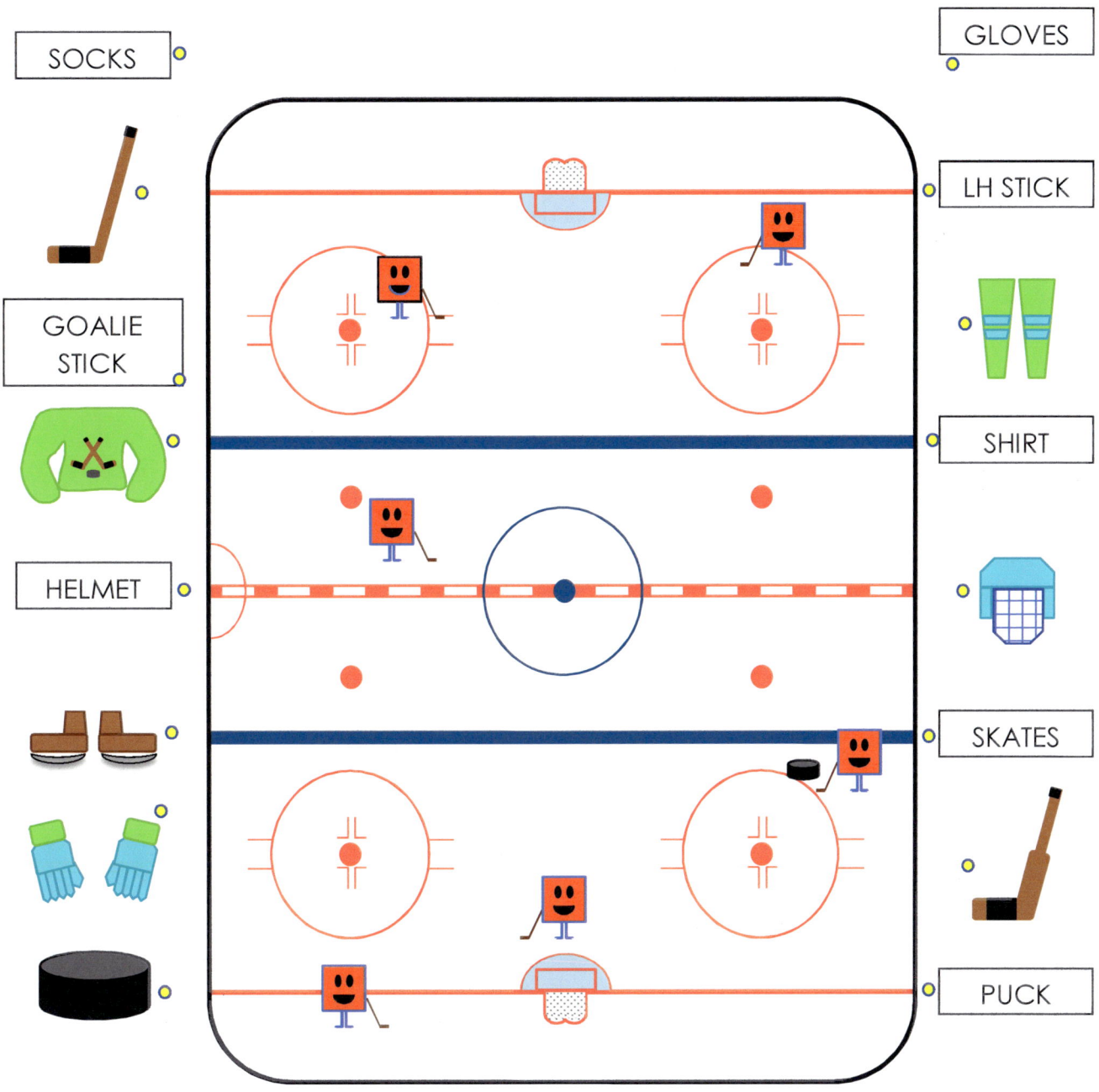

Page 23

PRACTICE: PROTECTIVE EQUIPMENT CROSSWORD

Solve the questions to fill in the Crossword Puzzle.

Across

2. Used to protect your hands.
4. Players shoot this into the net.
6. Protects your elbows.
7. Your team will have matching ones.
8. Put all the equipment into this to carry.
10. Careful because these are very sharp.
11. Sometimes this is made of wood.

Down

1. These pull up over top the shin guards.
3. Pads that make you look big and strong.
5. Keeps your head safe.
7. Wear these to go fast on the ice.
9. Wrap black or white around your stick.

The Players and Positions

When it is time to play the game, each team will put 5 players and 1 goalie on the ice. The 5 players are divided into 3 forward positions and 2 defensive positions. There will be 1 goalie to guard the net.

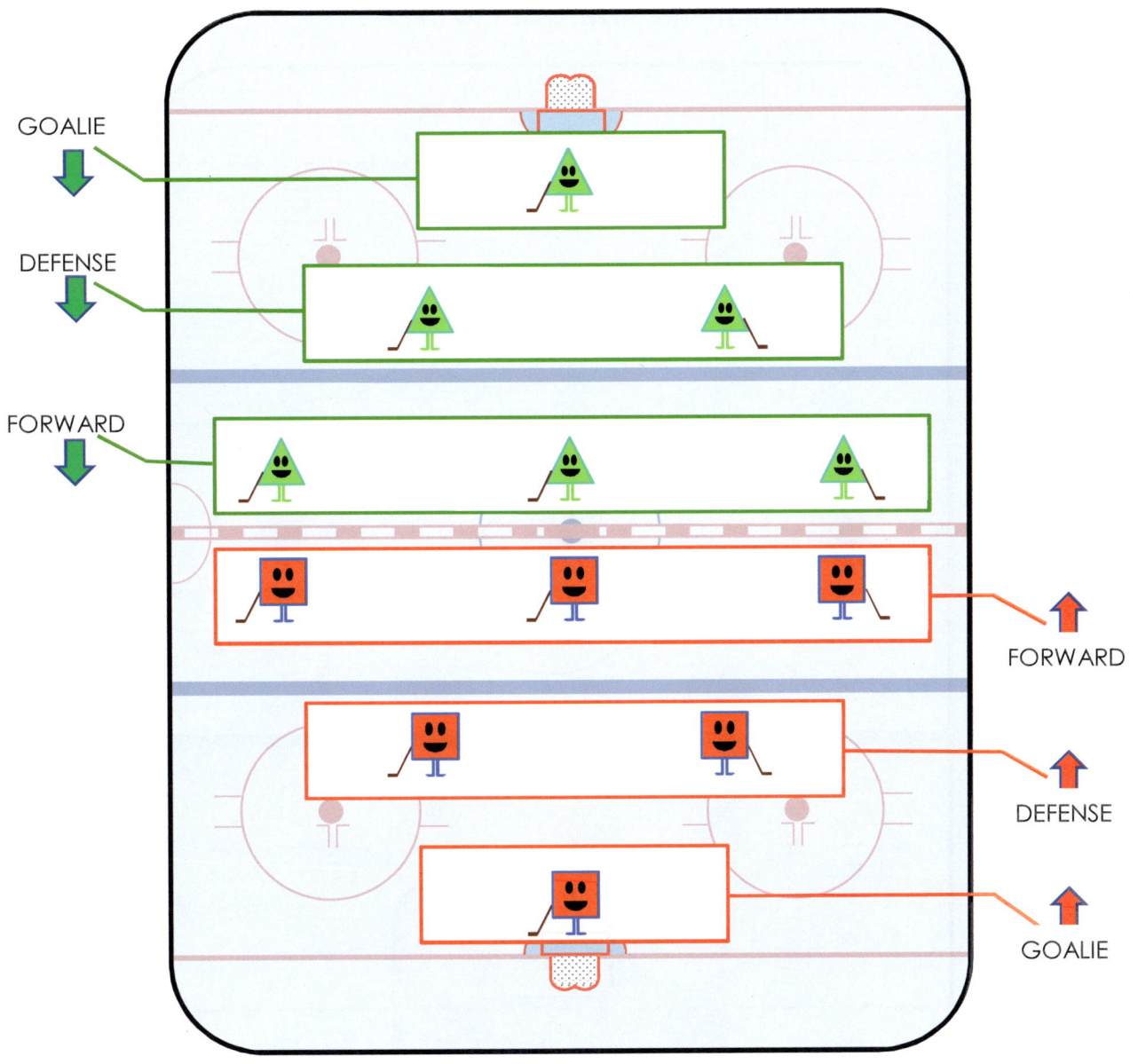

Using the team as an example, we will explain the player positions.

The Goalie

The job of the **GOALIE** is to protect the net. The goalie tries to keep the other team from getting the puck into the net. The goalie does this by standing in front of the net and **SAVING** or stopping the puck from entering the net by using their stick or body.

Area of Play
The goalie stays close to the net.

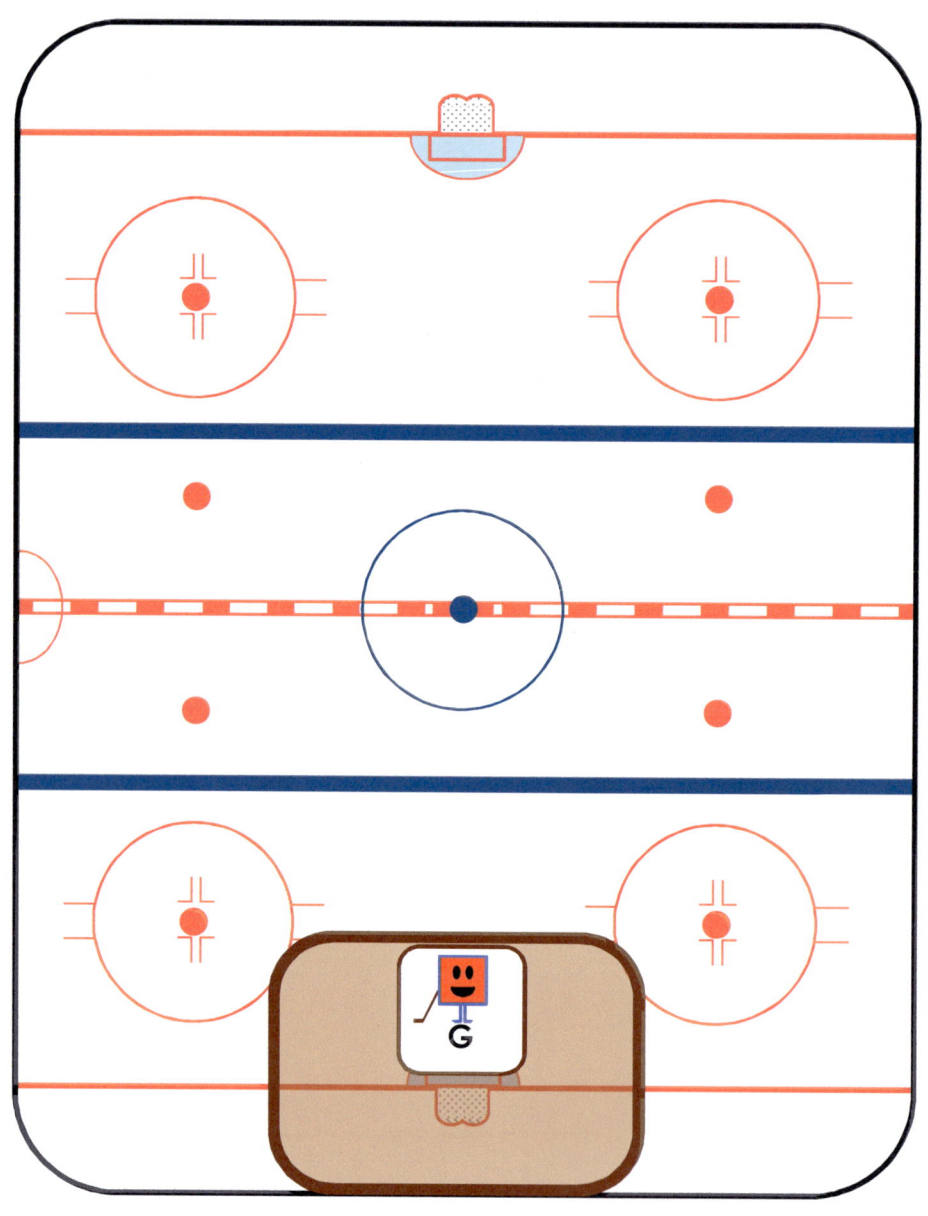

The Defense

The defense is made up of 2 players; the left defense, and the right defense.

The **LEFT DEFENSE** will play on the left side of the rink. **LD**

The **RIGHT DEFENSE** will play on the right side of the rink. **RD**

Areas of Play
All 2 Defense Positions LD and RD

Left Defense Area of Play

Right Defense Area of Play

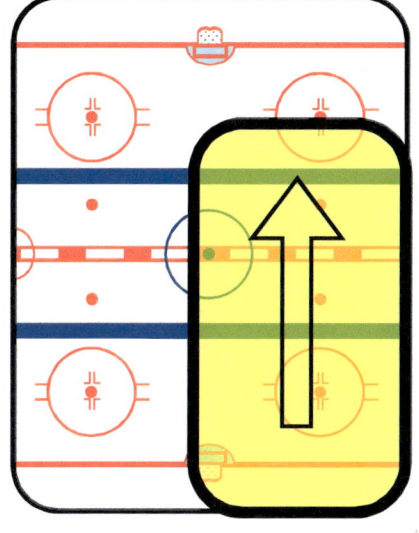

Here are all 2 Defense Positions LD and RD combined.

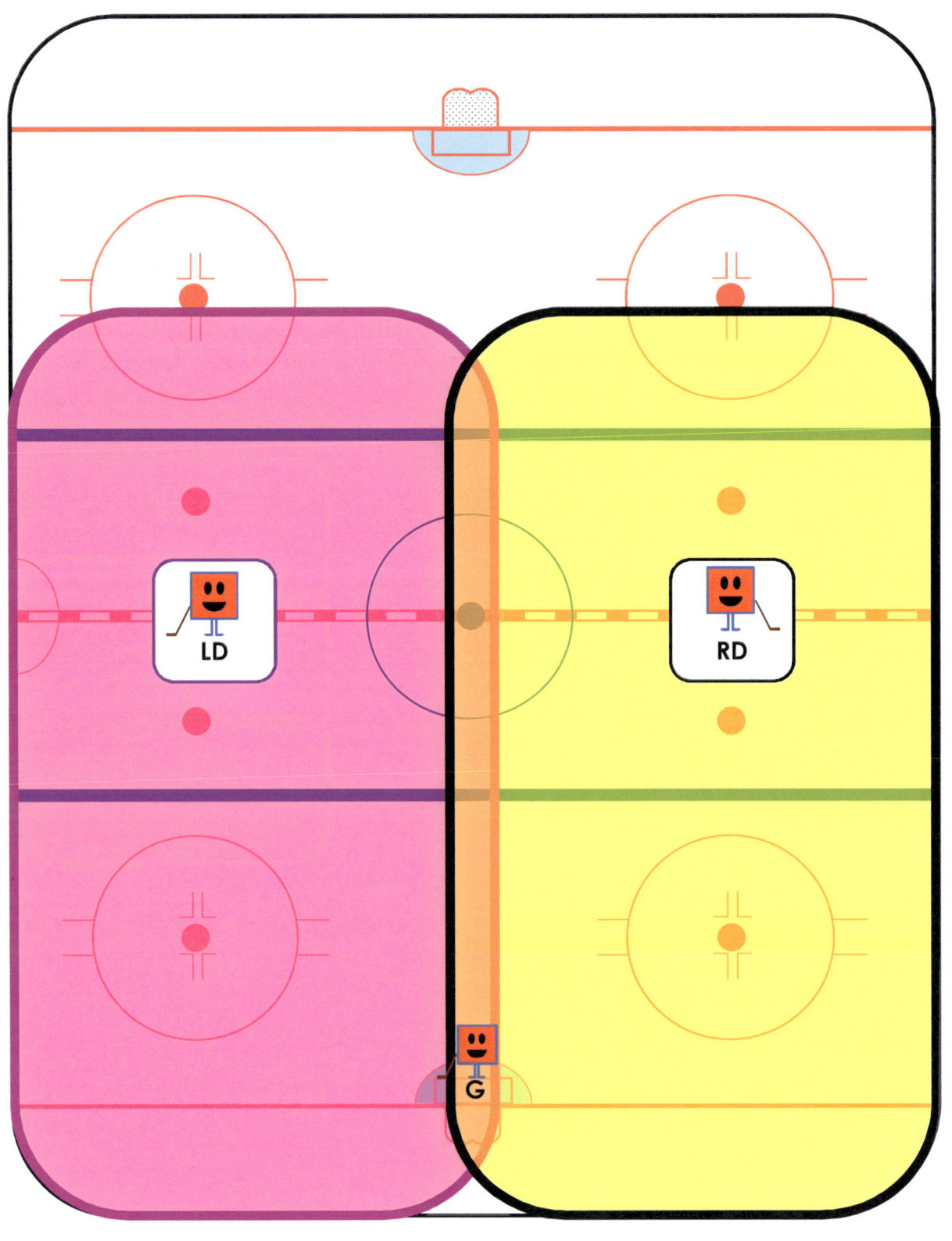

The Forwards

The **FORWARDS** or **OFFENSE** are made up of 3 players; the left wing, the center, and the right wing.

The **LEFT WING**, or **LEFT WINGER**, will play on the left side of the rink.

The **CENTER** will play in the center of the rink.

The **RIGHT WING**, or **RIGHT WINGER**, will play on the right side of the rink.

LW

C

RW

Areas of Play

All 3 Forward Positions LW, C, RW

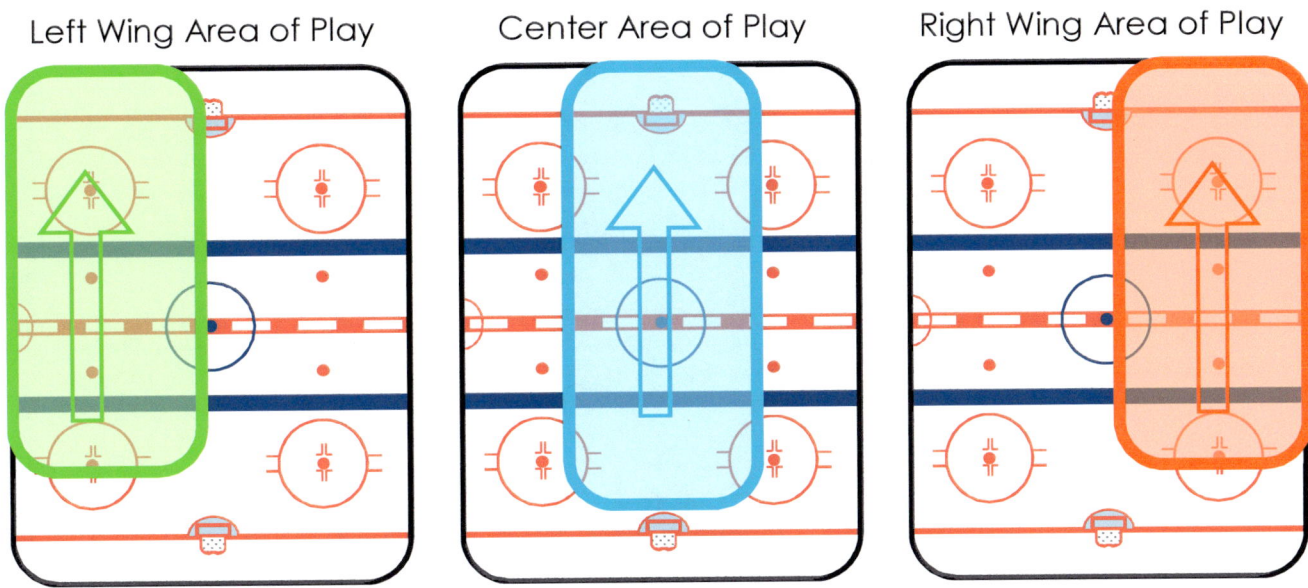

Left Wing Area of Play   Center Area of Play   Right Wing Area of Play

Here are all 3 Forward Positions LW, C, RW combined.

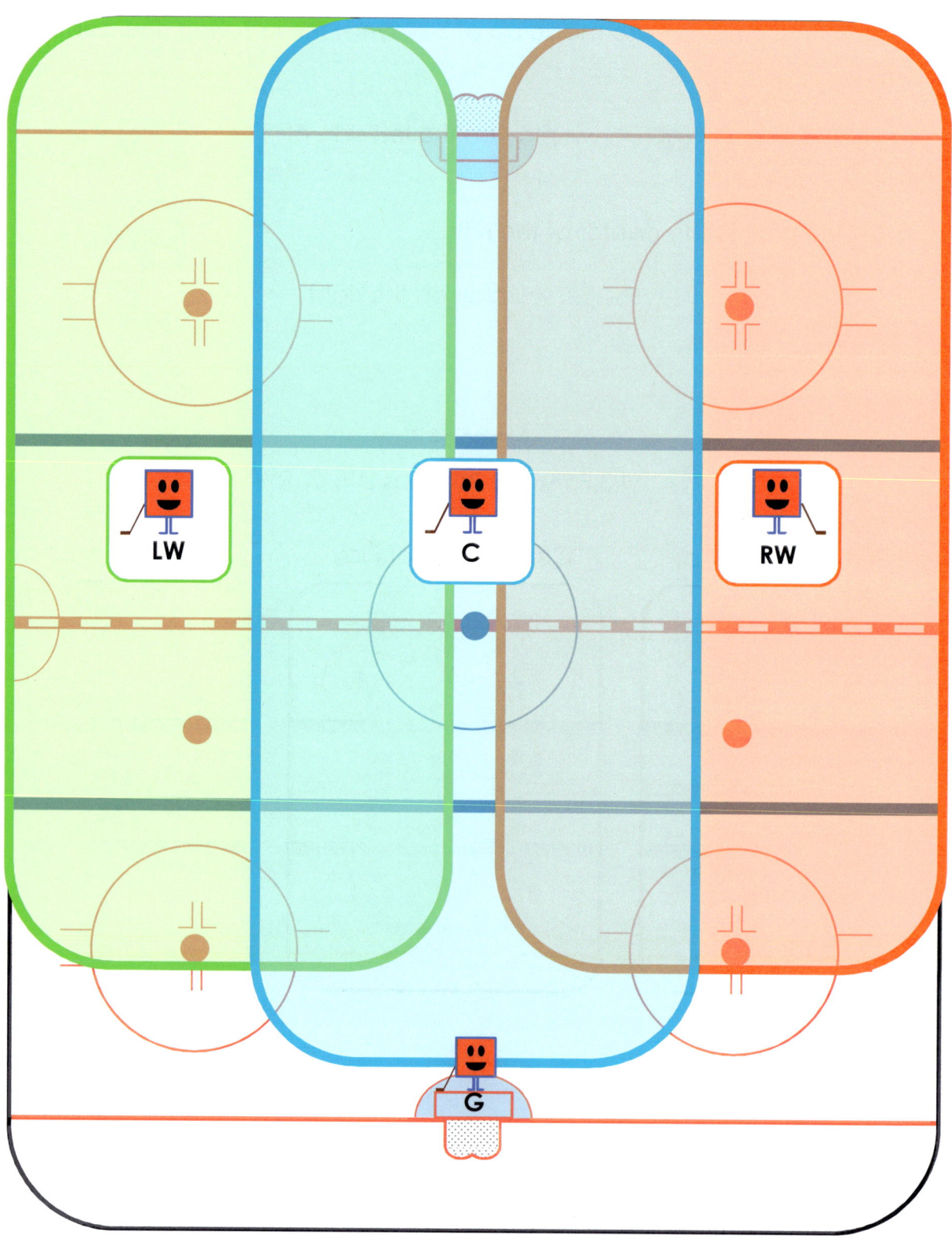

Playing Your Position

It is important that all the players on a hockey team play their position. Playing the correct position helps everyone to work together. When one player is not playing their position it is harder for the team to control the puck.

A hockey player who is not in the area of the puck and is waiting for someone to pass them the puck is sometimes called a **CHERRY PICKER**. Usually, it is not nice to be a cherry picker because they are not helping their team to get the puck.

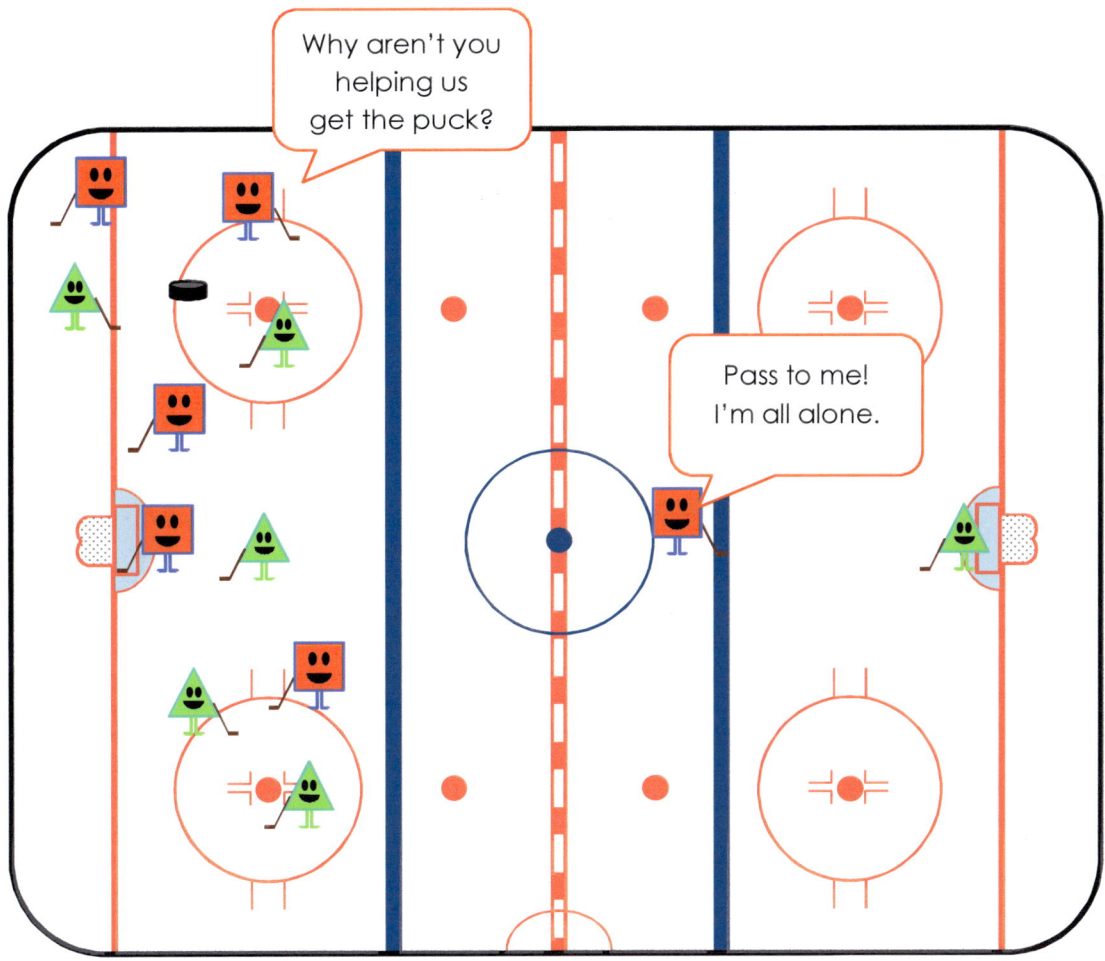

Practice: Forwards and Positions

Draw an arrow to show which player should be covering the position.

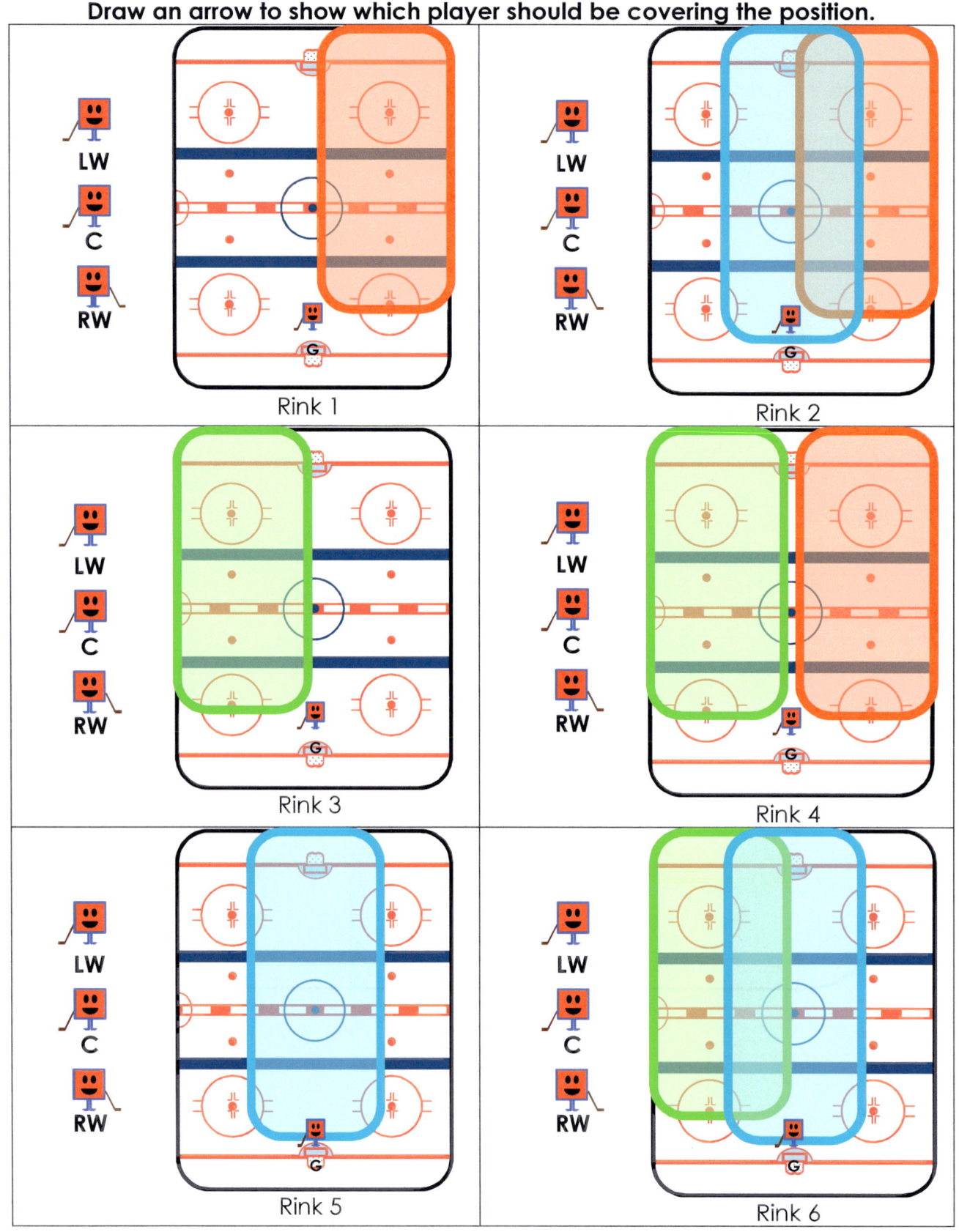

PRACTICE: WHO IS NOT IN THE CORRECT POSITION

Circle the player who is NOT in the correct position?
Draw and ARROW to where they should be.
HINT: Imagine the area the player is supposed to be in.

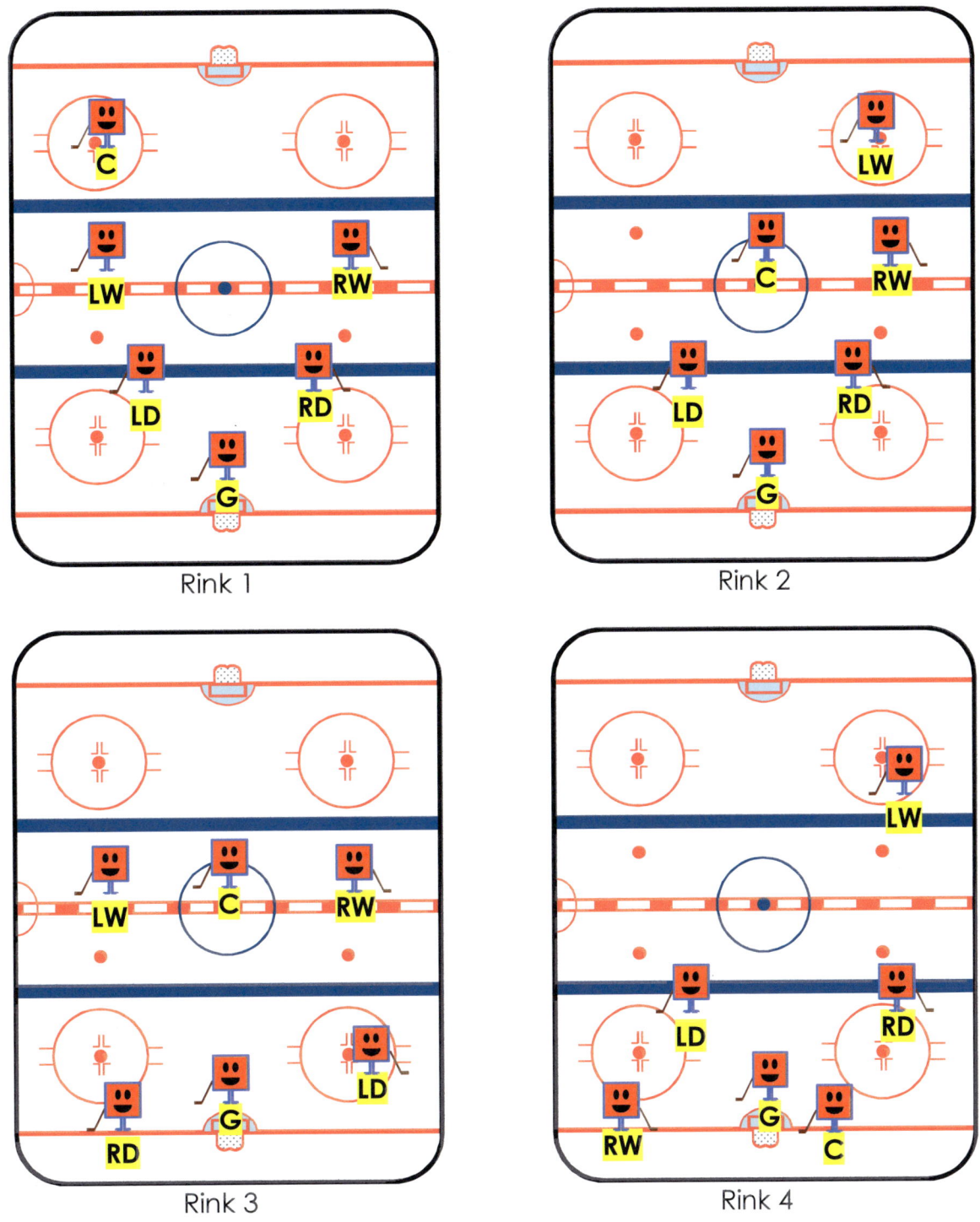

Rink 1

Rink 2

Rink 3

Rink 4

PRACTICE: WHO IS NOT IN THE CORRECT POSITION

Circle the player who is NOT in the correct position?
Draw and ARROW to where they should be.
HINT: The Goalie is always in the correct position.

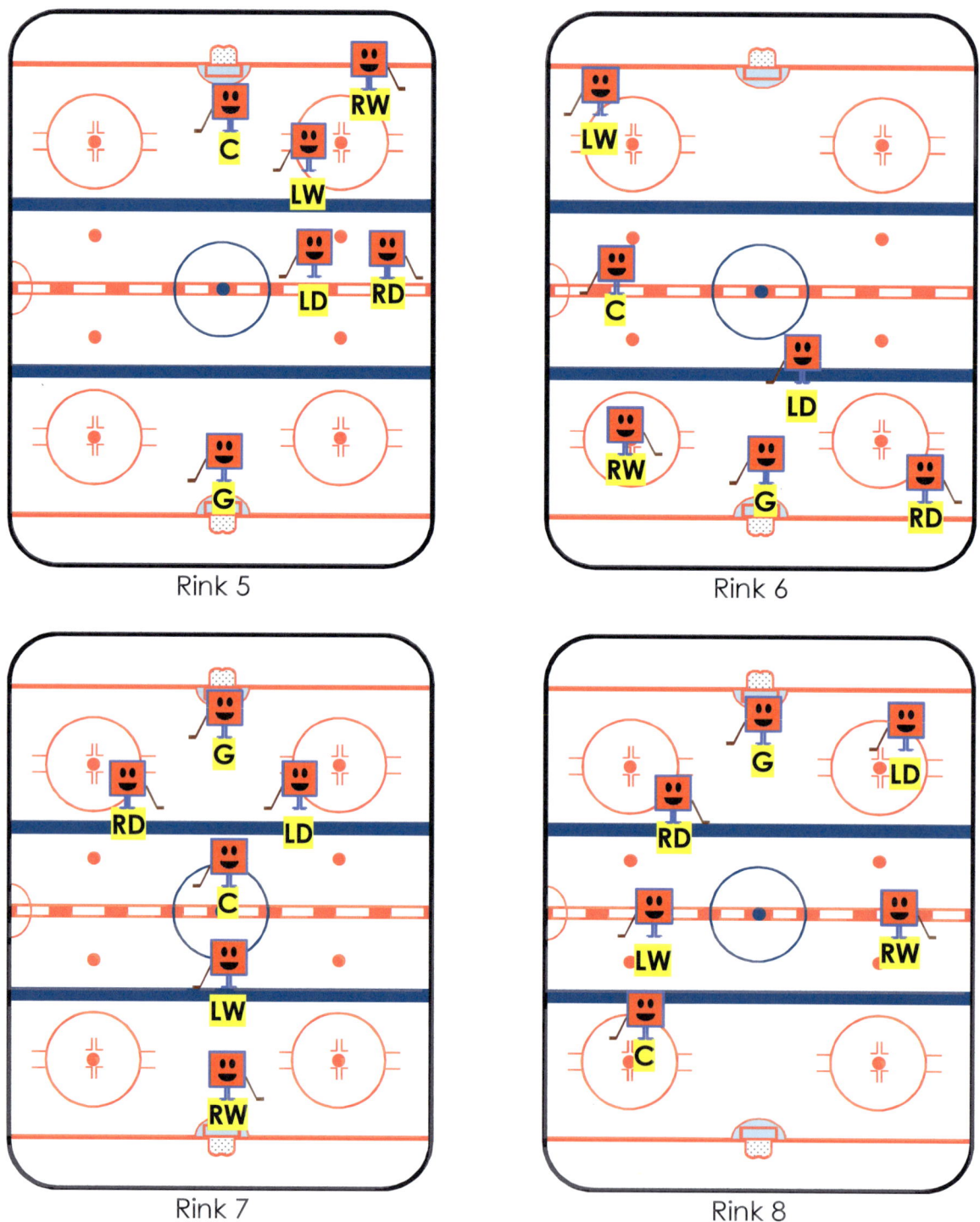

Rink 5

Rink 6

Rink 7

Rink 8

THE GAME

Starting the Game

A hockey game begins with 1 goalie and 5 players from each team on the ice. Each team has their players on the half of the ice where their team bench is. The goalies stand in their goalie crease in front of their net. The players line up for a face-off at center ice. The Referee will drop the puck on the center ice dot to start the game.

Starting the Game at Center Ice

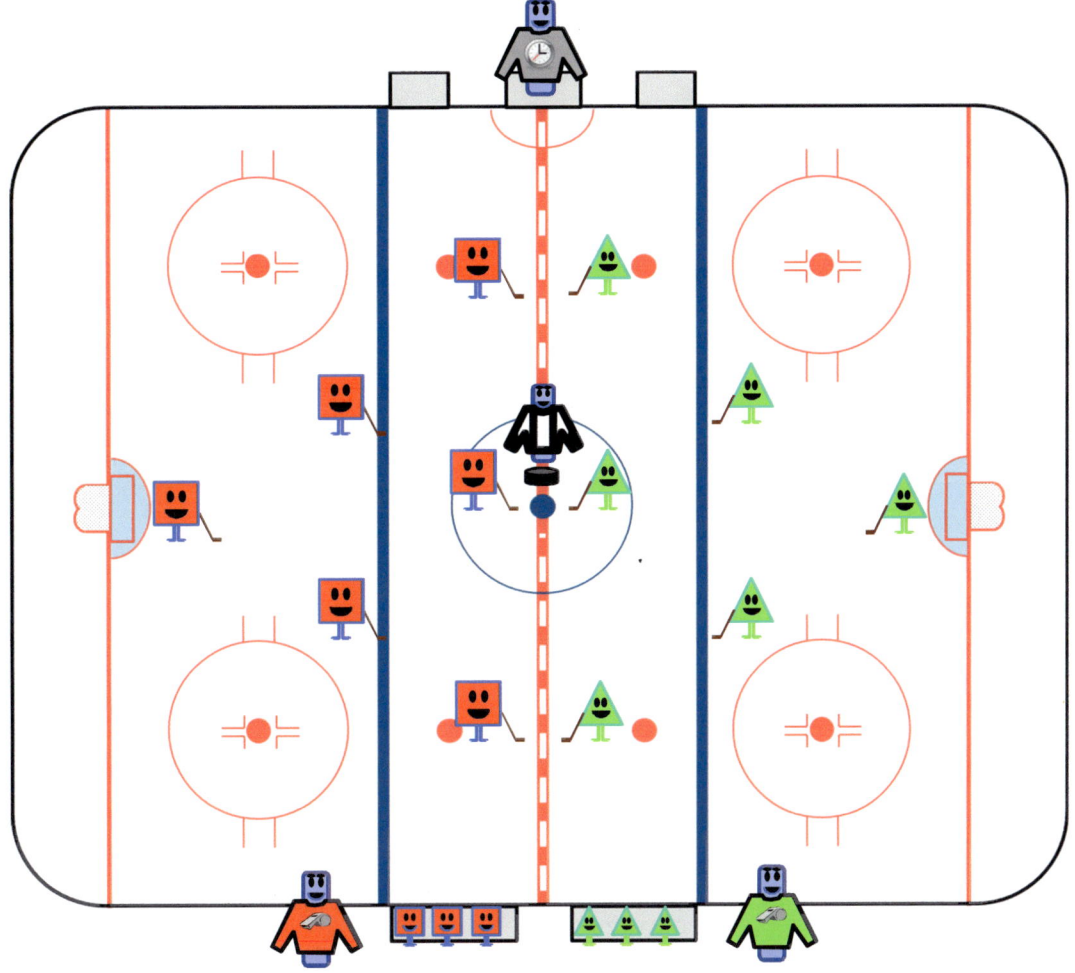

Starting a Face-Off

When the Referee blows the whistle to stop the game, the game will start again with a face-off. The Referee will decide which dot to restart the game at, based on why the game was stopped. The Referee might hold up his hand with the puck to show the hockey players which dot the game will restart at.

The Center: Only the Center is allowed at the dot. The 2 Centers face each other at the dot and stand still waiting for the puck to drop. When the puck drops, the center player tries to pass the puck BEHIND them to one of the players on their team.

The Right Wing / Left Wing: The left and right wing players line up at the hash marks facing their opponent. Their skates cannot go into the circle or over the hash mark.

The Right Defense and Left Defense: The right and left defense players line up behind the circle. Their skates cannot go into the circle.

Players Line Up for a Face-Off

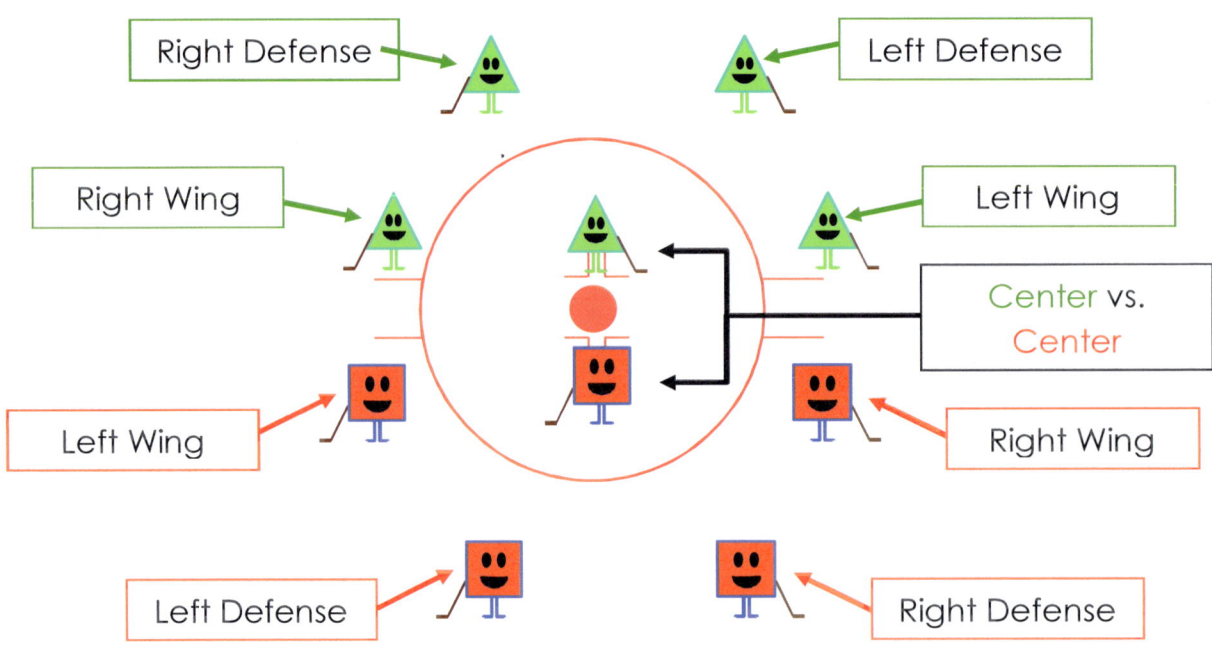

PRACTICE: START THE GAME

Help the people find where to go so the game can start.

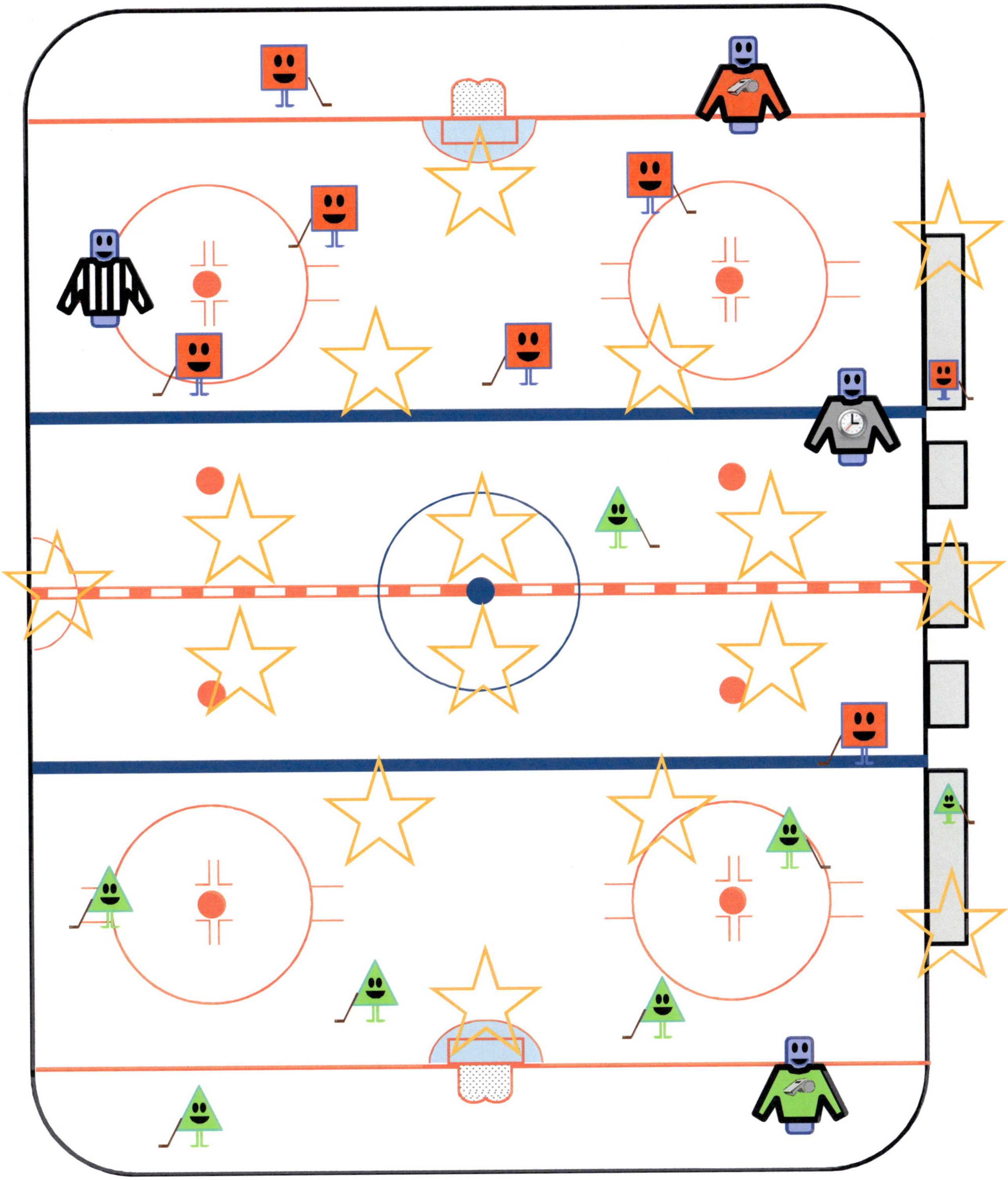

Page 37

Scoring

Hockey players try to **SHOOT** the puck into the other team's net to **SCORE** a goal. If a hockey player shoots the puck to someone on their own team, it is called a **PASS**. If a player shoots the puck, and the puck bounces off the goalie, it is called a **REBOUND**.

Each team will try and SHOOT the PUCK into the other team's NET. If the puck completely crosses the goal line, and goes into the NET, then that team will have **SCORED A GOAL**. The Timekeeper will add 1 **POINT** for the team that scored the goal. Be careful not to score a goal on your own net, because if you do, the other team will get awarded one point.

If a goalie stops all the shots in a game and has zero goals scored against them, the Coach will say that the goalie got a **SHUT OUT**.

If one player scores 3 goals in a single game, the Coach will say that the player got a **HAT TRICK**. The fans might throw their hats on the ice to celebrate.

If a player can get the puck, and get away from all the other players, and has a chance to score, all alone, then the player has a **BREAK AWAY**.

The SQUARE team player got the puck and is on a BREAK AWAY.

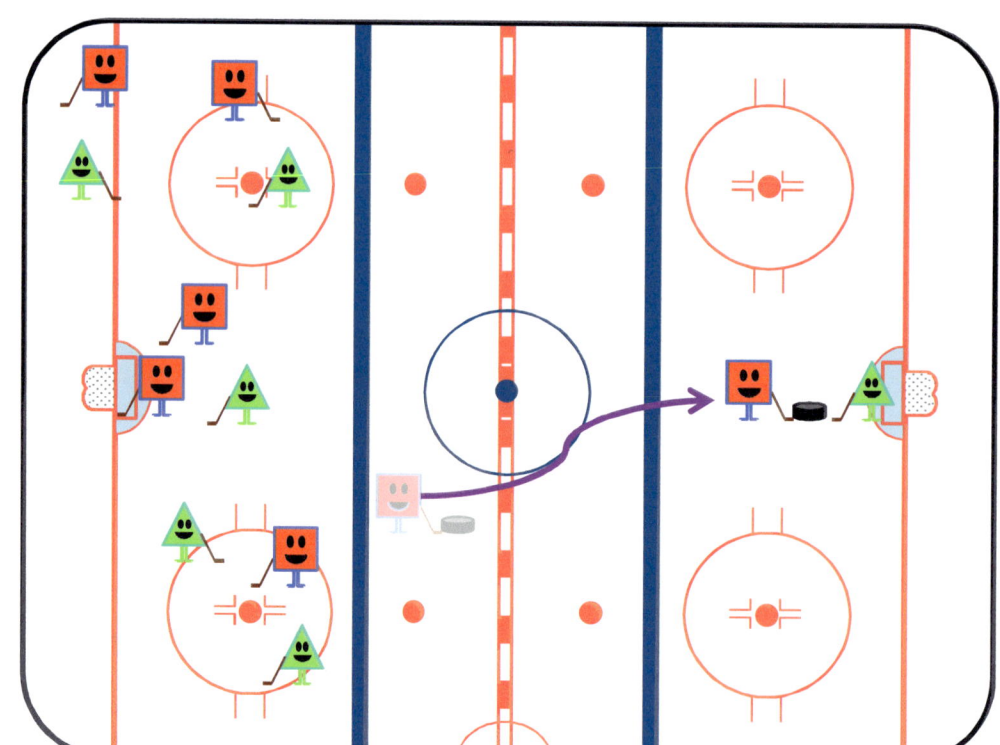

Practice: Break Away Maze
Score on a Break Away

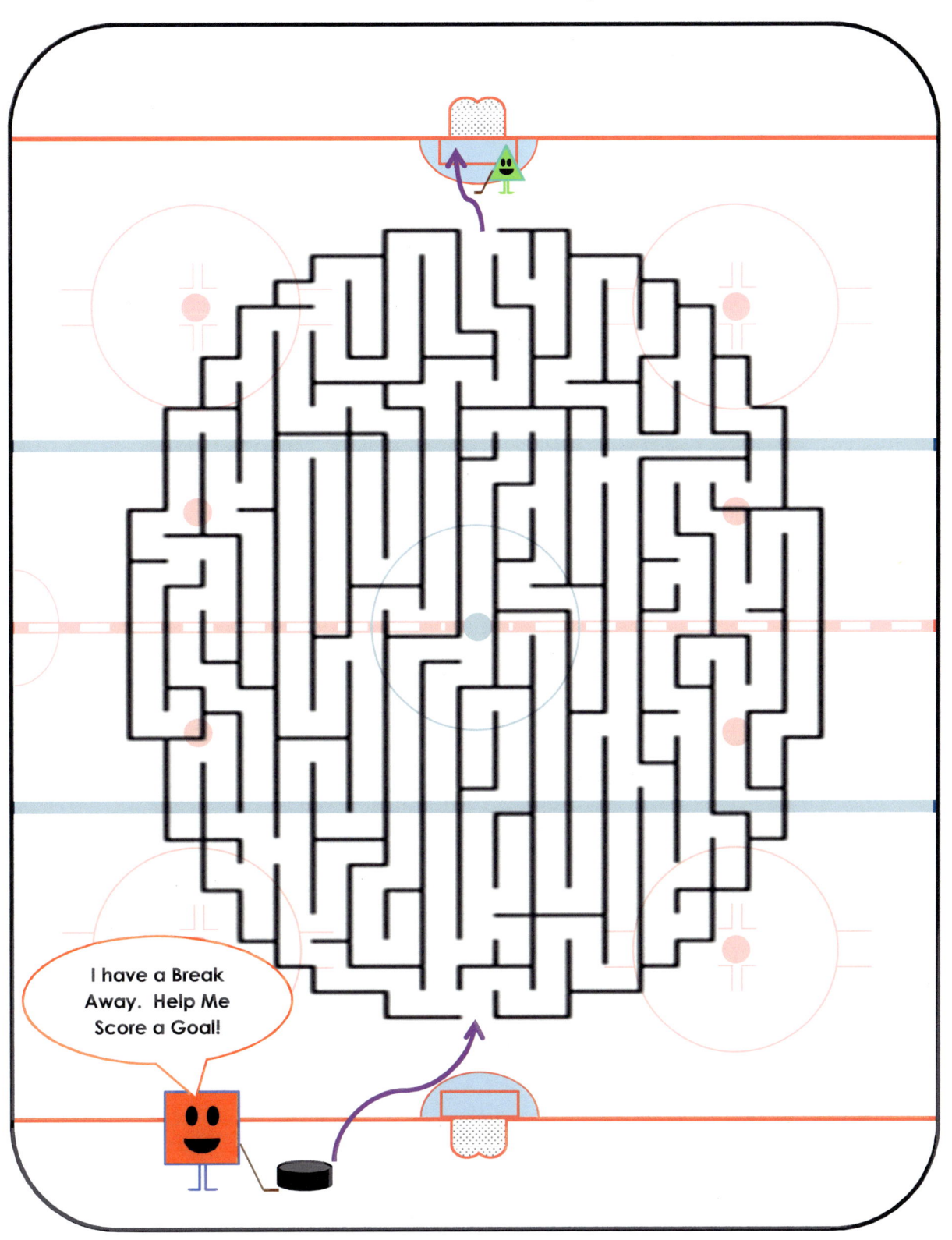

Keeping Time

A hockey game is played for 60 minutes. The 60 minutes are divided into 3 *PERIODS*. The periods are called the *1st PERIOD*, the *2nd PERIOD*, and the *3rd PERIOD*. Each period is 20 minutes long. The period starts at 20 minutes and counts down to 0 minutes. At the end of each period a buzzer will sound and the goalies will switch sides, and each team will play in the opposite direction.

The Score Board

From the *SCORE BOARD* below, you can see:

- There are 12 minutes and 37 seconds left in the period. The Score Board starts each period at 20:00 minutes and counts down to 0:00.
- It is period number 3. It is the 3rd period.
- The Home team has scored 2 goals.
- The Visitor team has scored 1 goal.
- The Home team has 1 player in the penalty box with 1 minute and 14 seconds left in the penalty. The penalty time counts down to zero.
- The Visitor team has 2 players in the penalty box. There is 1 minute and 14 seconds left in the first penalty. There are 45 seconds left in the second penalty.

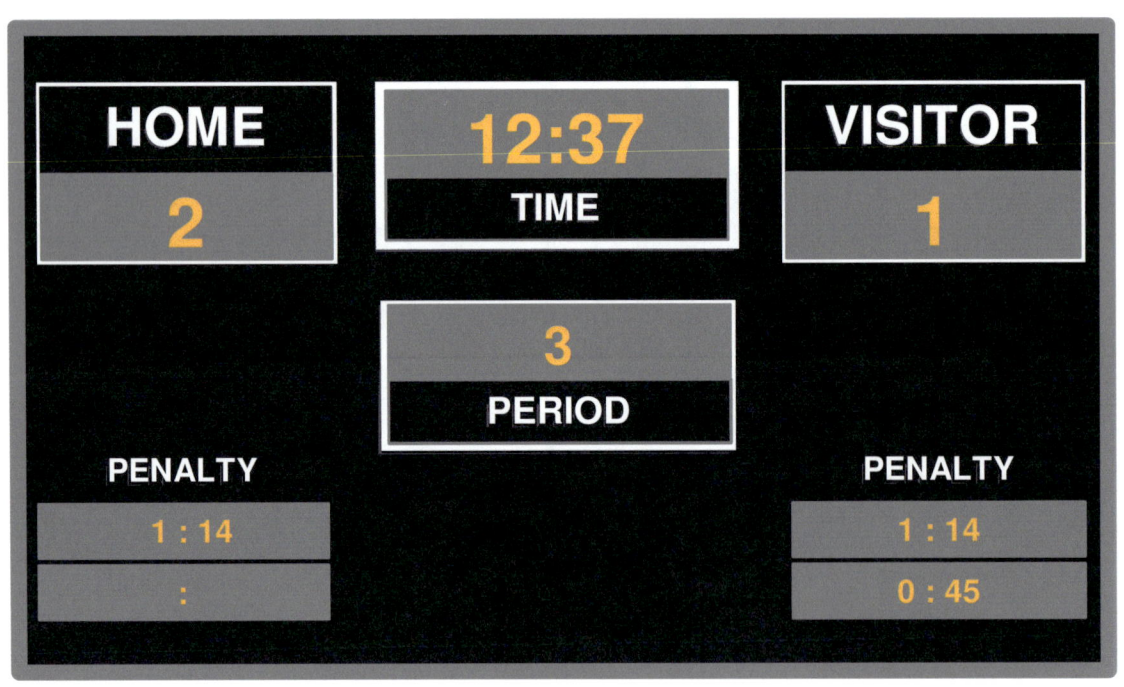

Telling the Score

When telling a game score, the highest number of goals is mentioned first. For example, if the Home team has 1 goal and the Visitor team has 3 goals, the score is "3 to 1 for the VISITOR team". If the two teams have the same number of goals, it is called a **TIE GAME**.

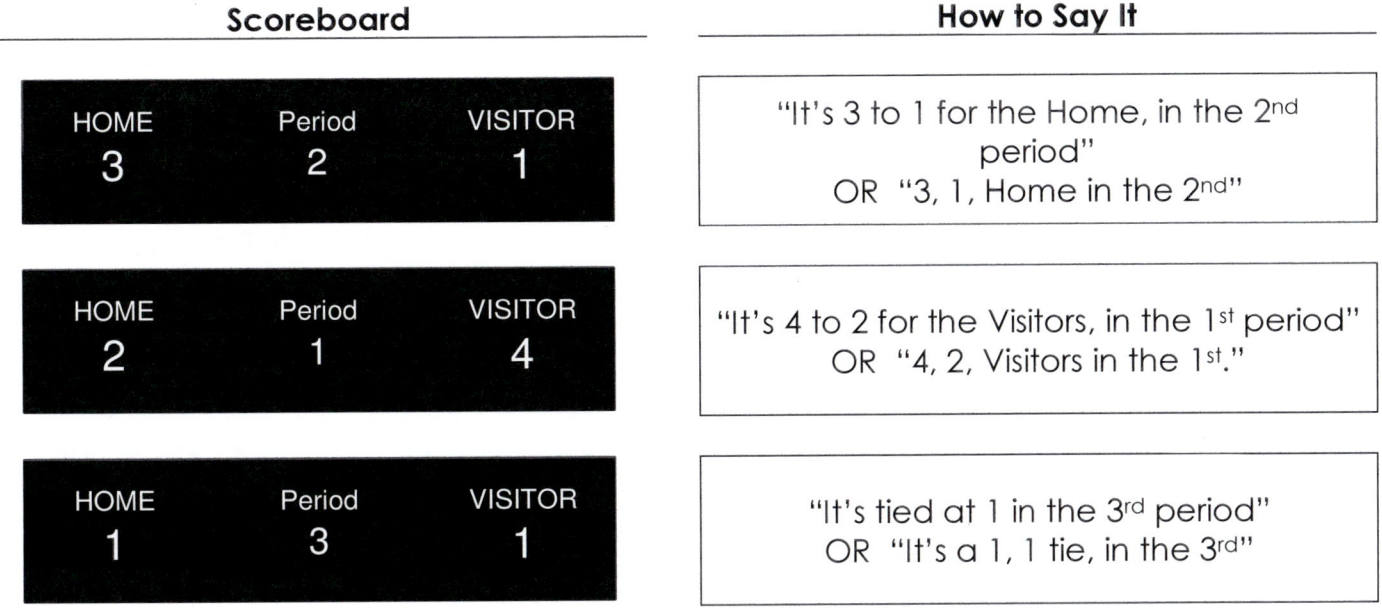

Versus

In hockey we say that one team **VERSUS** another team. That means the two teams are playing against each other. The short form for the word versus is the two letters vs.

The standard way to say that two teams are playing against each other is to say the VISITOR TEAM vs. THE HOME TEAM. It's easy to remember that versus can be replaced by "is playing at". Now you can say the VISITOR TEAM is playing at the HOME TEAM.

Winning

The team with the most goals at the end of the 3rd PERIOD will **WIN THE GAME**. During some special types of games, if at the end of the 3rd period the score is tied, then the game can continue into more periods. The extra periods are called **OVERTIME**. An overtime period comes to an end as soon as one team scores another goal.

At the end of a hockey game the entire team will go on the ice and surround their goalie and congratulate one another. Then both teams will line up at center ice to shake hands. Shaking hands at the end of a game is a tradition in hockey. It shows that no matter which team won, and no matter what hard feelings might have happened during the game, all the players can be friends after the game is done. When shaking hands, each player will normally say "**GOOD GAME**" to the other player. Even the Coaches come on the ice to shake hands.

Practice: Word Find with Mystery Code

Do the word find and solve the mystery code

H	O	C	R	K	E	E	Z	Y	I	S	F	T	S	U
N	T	O	P	E	M	P	L	O	Y	A	O	Y	H	P
X	G	Q	T	A	B	G	O	A	N	O	E	H	U	U
D	L	V	G	H	A	O	W	I	H	E	X	S	T	V
A	E	E	F	X	A	A	U	S	N	W	S	E	O	Y
F	I	R	R	M	K	T	B	N	F	T	D	K	U	T
T	U	N	O	A	Z	Y	T	X	D	L	R	X	T	D
K	U	M	E	C	S	G	E	R	E	O	G	O	L	T
T	Y	R	A	Y	S	Z	B	G	I	S	S	V	B	V
H	B	G	O	O	D	G	A	M	E	C	B	E	E	L
D	R	C	O	R	E	J	O	T	S	Z	K	R	X	F
P	E	R	I	O	D	S	P	A	S	S	W	T	F	T
G	F	X	R	Q	V	A	Q	C	V	K	X	I	G	O
V	Z	I	S	I	L	B	K	X	H	Z	J	M	D	N
U	S	C	O	R	E	B	O	A	R	D	U	E	T	H

BREAK AWAY   PERIODS   SHOOT
GOOD GAME   POINT   SHUT OUT
HAT TRICK   REBOUND   TIE GAME
OVERTIME   SCORE BOARD   ZONES
PASS   SCORED

__ __ __ __ __ __   __ __ __ __ __

   __ __   __ __ __ __

Solve the mystery code using the first letters NOT used.

Page 43

Zones

There are 3 areas of the ice rink that are called *ZONES*. The 2 zones on each end of the ice are sometimes called *END ZONES*. The zone in the middle of the ice is called the *NEUTRAL ZONE*.

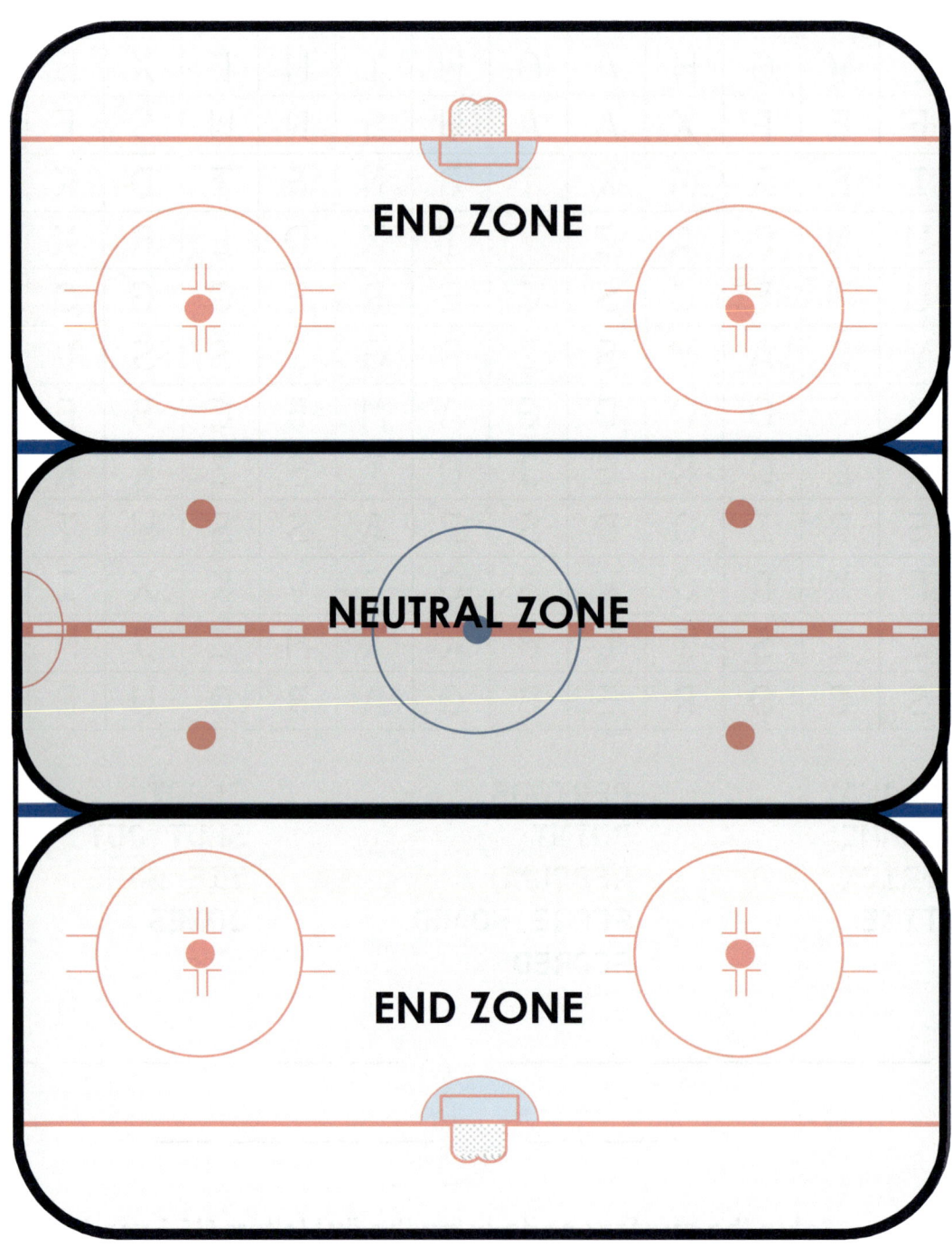

Each Coach will call the 3 zones the **OFFENSIVE ZONE**, the **NEURTAL ZONE**, and the **DEFENSIVE ZONE**. A hockey team will behave differently in each zone.

The **OFFENSIVE ZONE** is the area of ice where a hockey team is trying to score on the other team. It is between the blue line and the **other team's net**.

THE OFFENSIVE ZONE

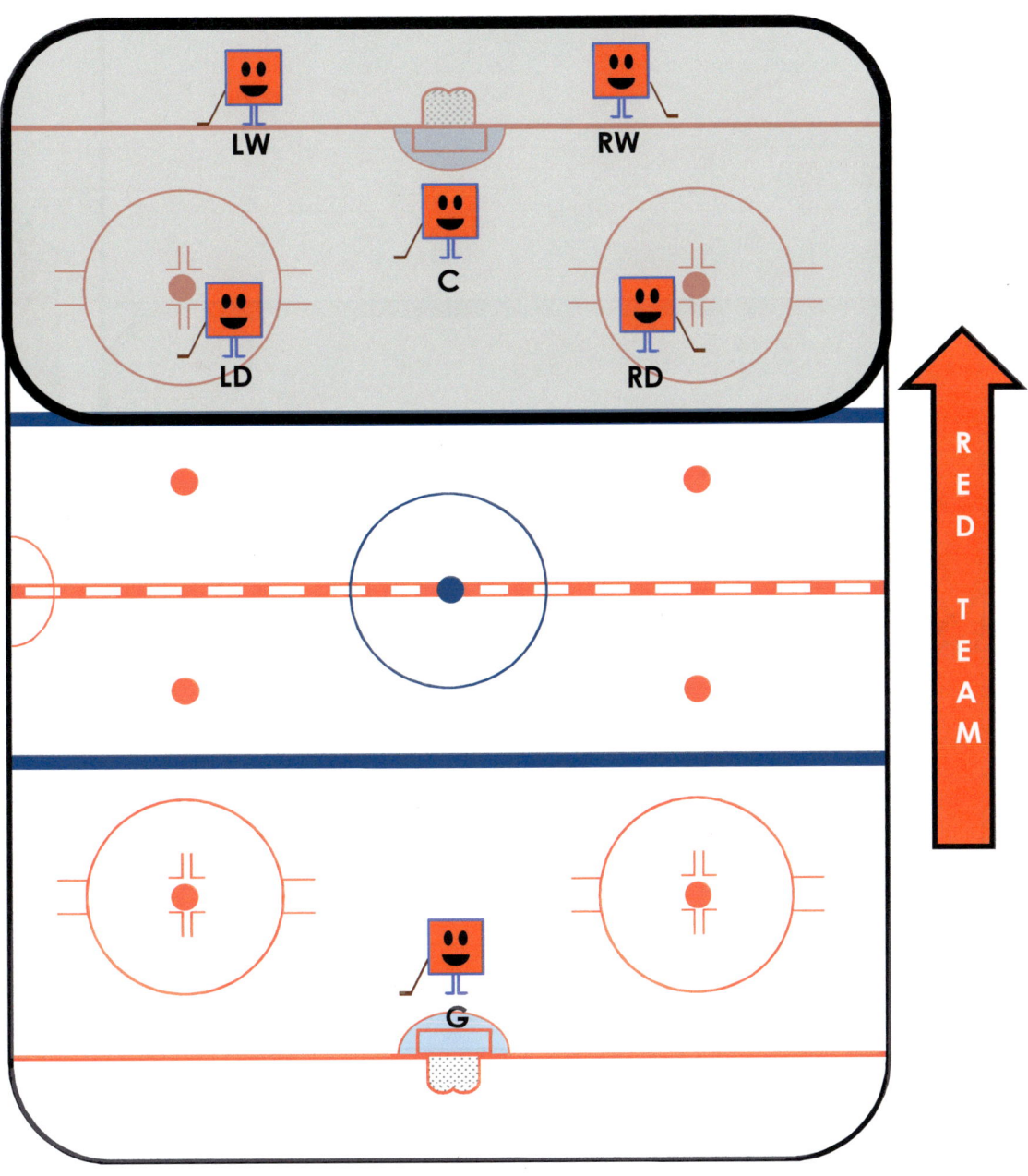

The **NEUTRAL ZONE** is the area of ice where a hockey team is trying to move forward. It is between the 2 blue lines. In the neurtral zone, each team is trying to get the puck.

THE NEUTRAL ZONE

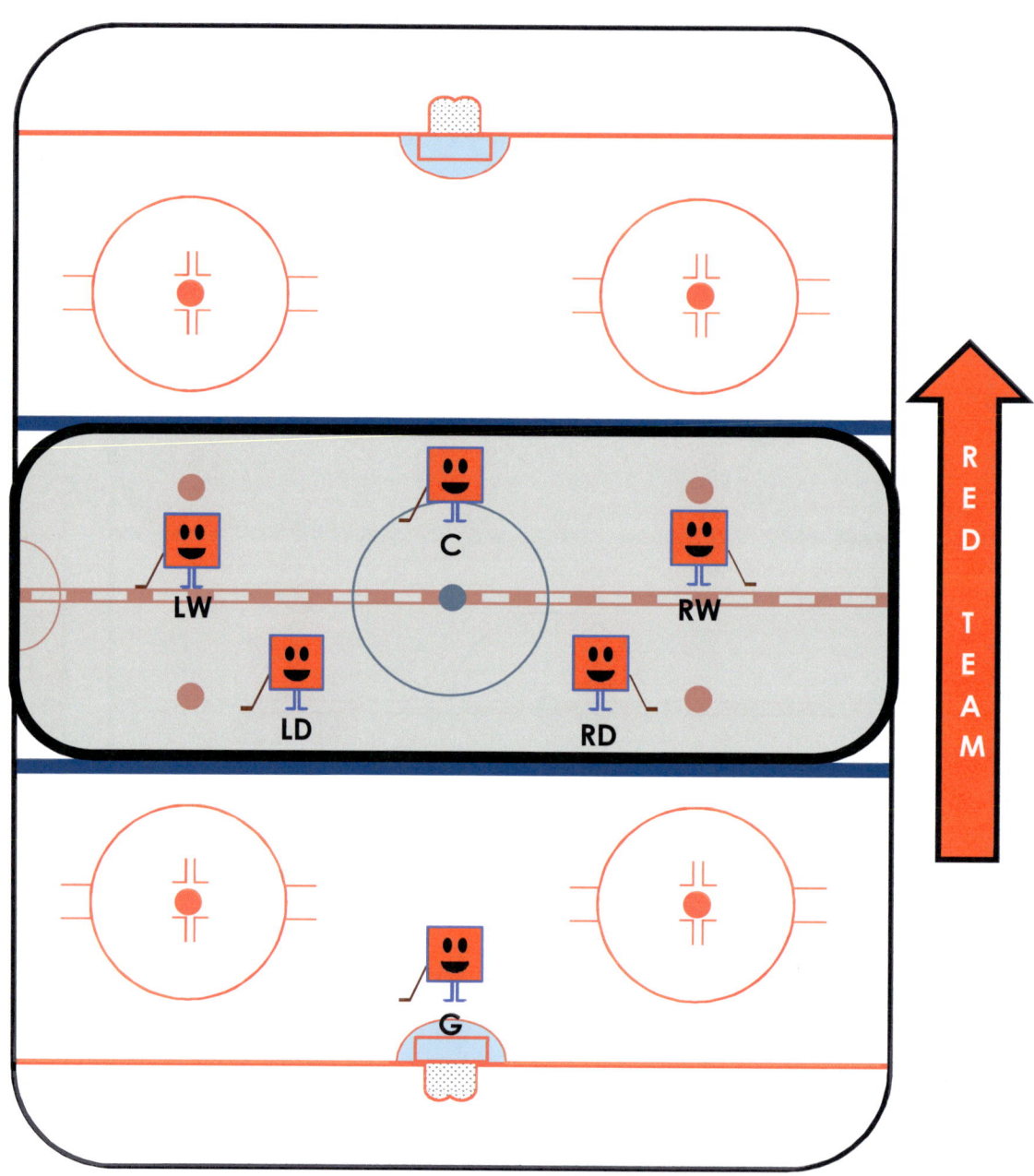

The **DEFENSIVE ZONE** is the area of ice where a hockey team is trying to stop the other team from scoring. It is between the blue line and **their own team's net**.

THE DEFENSIVE ZONE

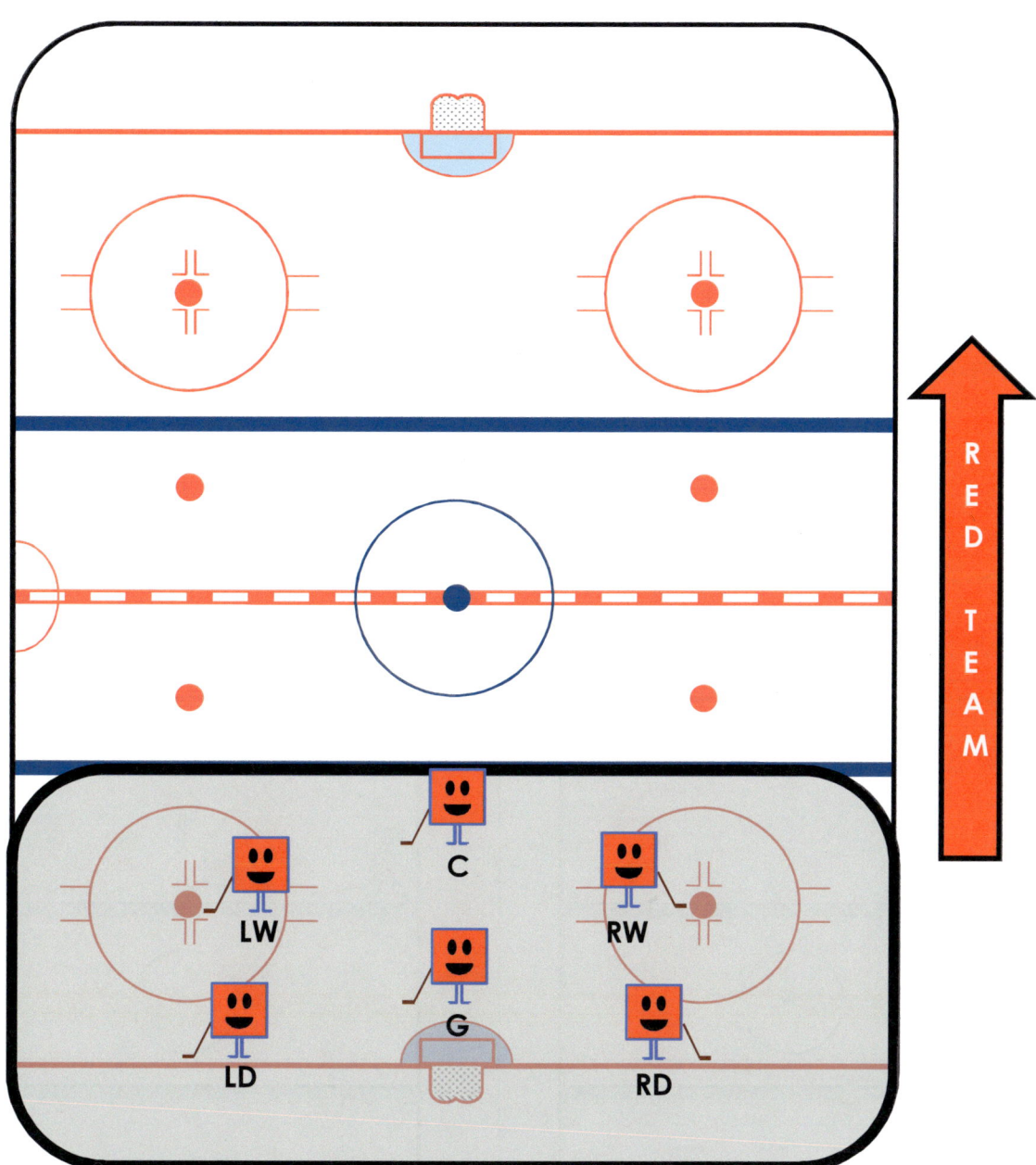

NOTICE THE DIFFERENCES

When one team is trying to score, the other team is trying to stop them from scoring. One team is in their Offensive Zone and the other team is in their Defensive Zone. The zone with your goalie is your Defensive Zone. The zone with the other team's goalie is your Offensive Zone.

PRACTICE: KNOW THE ZONES
Which Zone is each team in?

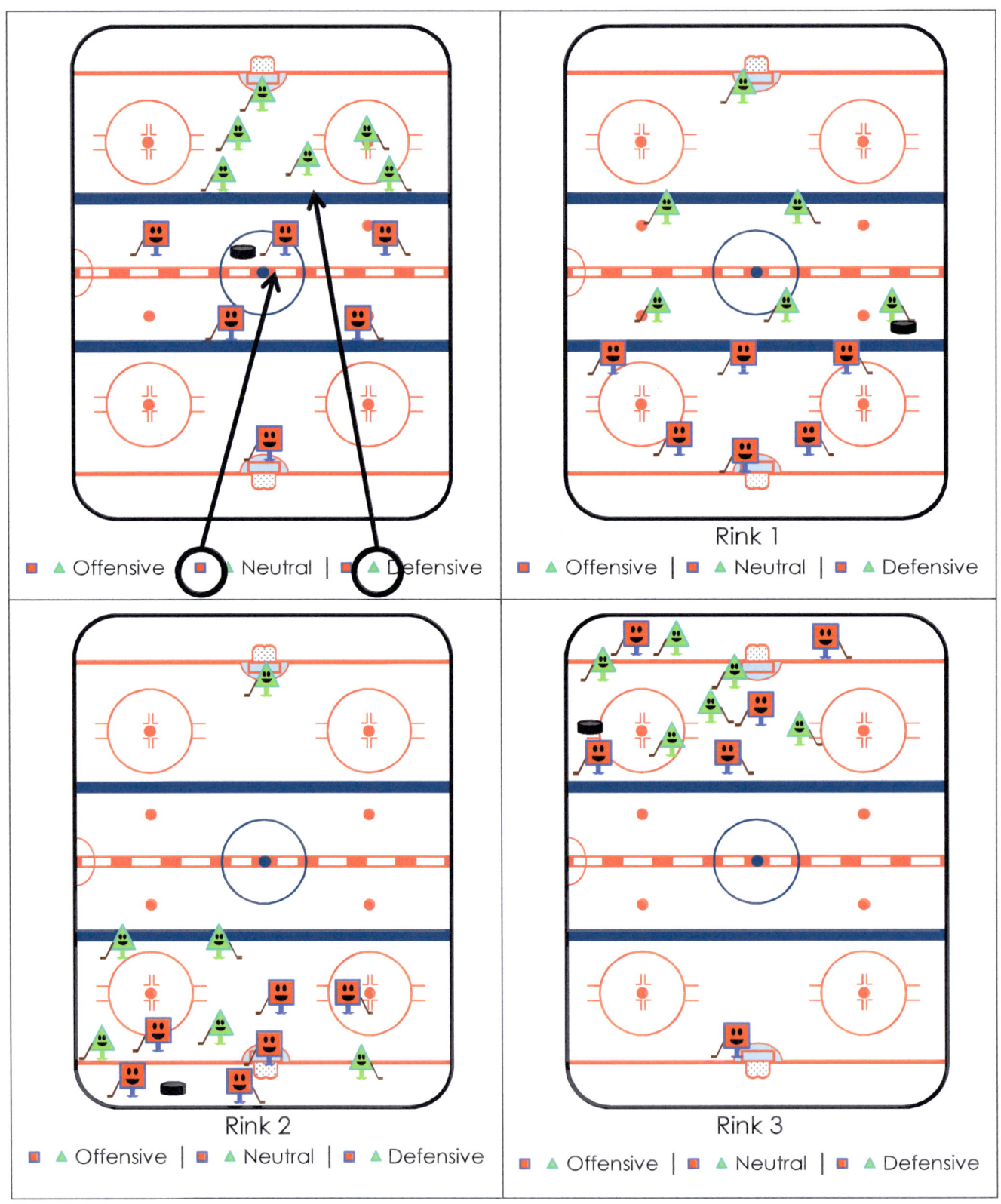

Page 48

PRACTICE: STAY IN THE CORRECT ZONE

Which Zone is each team in?
Also, circle the player who is NOT in the correct zone with his team?

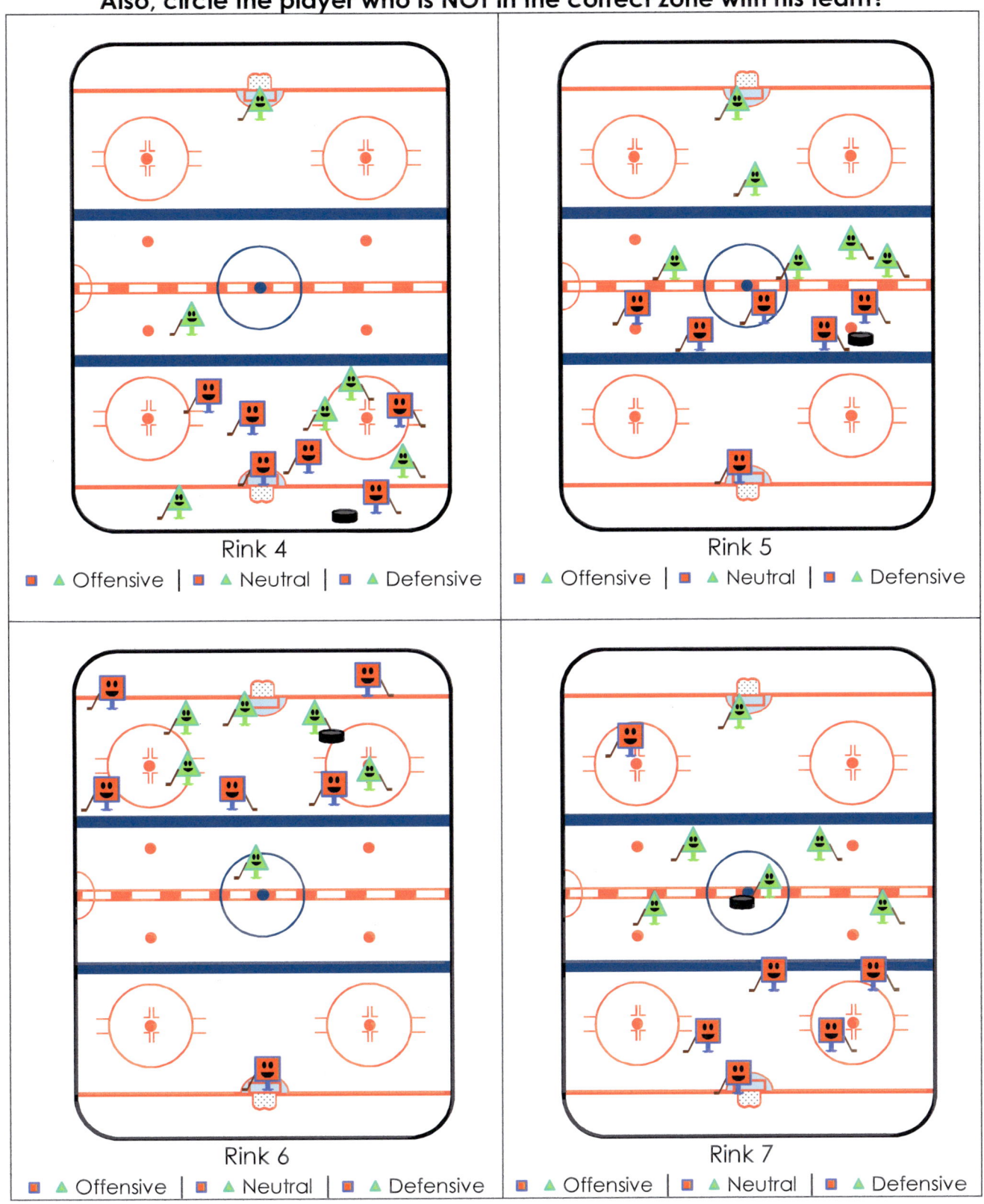

Fun Page

Draw a picture of a hockey player shooting on a goalie and scoring.

Send it to Coach John and we might put it on our website
www.HockeyCoachJohn.com
(Ask a parent)

THE RULES

To make hockey fair, each team must follow the rules. Referees are responsible for enforcing the rules. If a rule is broken the Referee will blow a whistle to stop the game.

When a "line" rule is broken the Line Referee, or **LINESMAN**, will blow the whistle, get the puck, and bring it back to one of the dots on the ice. The game will start again at the dot the Referee goes to for a face-off.

Icing

The **ICING** rule is to stop one team from shooting the puck all the way down the ice to the other team's side. A good hockey team is supposed to skate with the puck, pass to their teammates, and move the puck to the other team's side.

READ SLOWLY: If a team shoots the puck across the middle red line all the way down and over the other team's goal line, without anyone touching the puck, the Referee will blow the whistle. The team that shot the puck will be called for **ICING THE PUCK**.

The Referee will get the puck and bring it all the way back down the ice for a face-off. This is to teach the team the lesson that they are supposed to skate and pass the puck down the ice, and not just shoot it to the other team's side.

The red team shoots the puck too far.
It's ICING and the Referee brings the puck back.

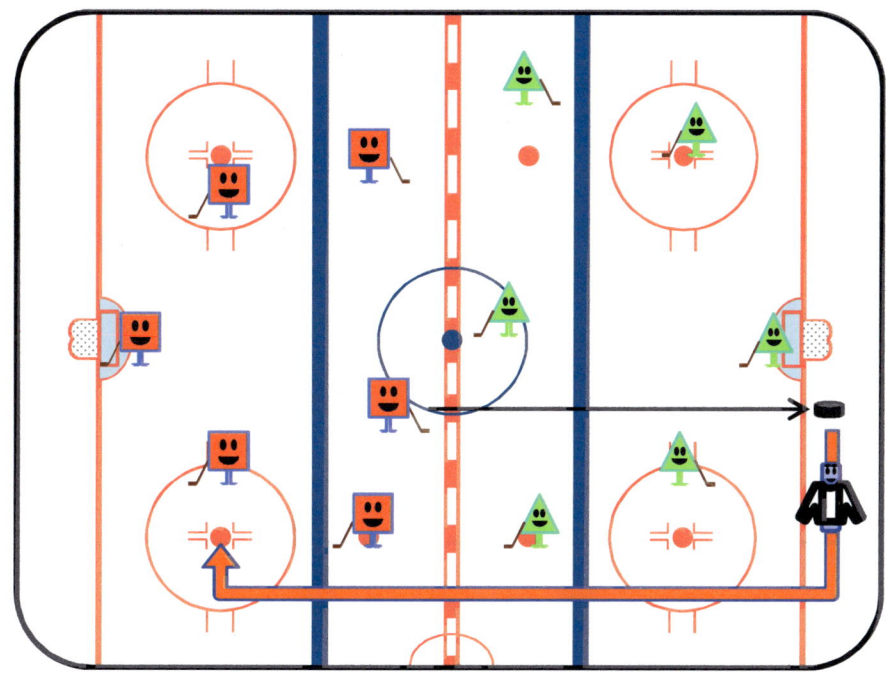

Off-side

The *OFF-SIDE* rule stops a team from keeping one of their players in front of the other team's goalie, waiting there for someone to pass the puck to them.

READ SLOWLY: When an attacking team has the puck in the Neutral Zone and wants to enter the Offensive Zone, they must make sure that the puck crosses over the blue line into the Offensive Zone before ANY of their players enter the Offensive Zone. The defending team can move from the Neutral Zone to their Defensive Zone any time they want.

If you are trying to score, the puck MUST cross the Offensive Zone blue line before anyone on your team does. If one or more players enter the Offensive Zone before the puck, the Referee will blow the whistle and stop the game. That team will be Off-Side. The Referee will bring the puck back to the nearest dot outside the blue line for a face-off.

The Right Wing for the TRIANGLE team is OFF SIDE.

Practice: You Make the Call

CIRCLE the correct answer. Be careful of Off-side and Icing.

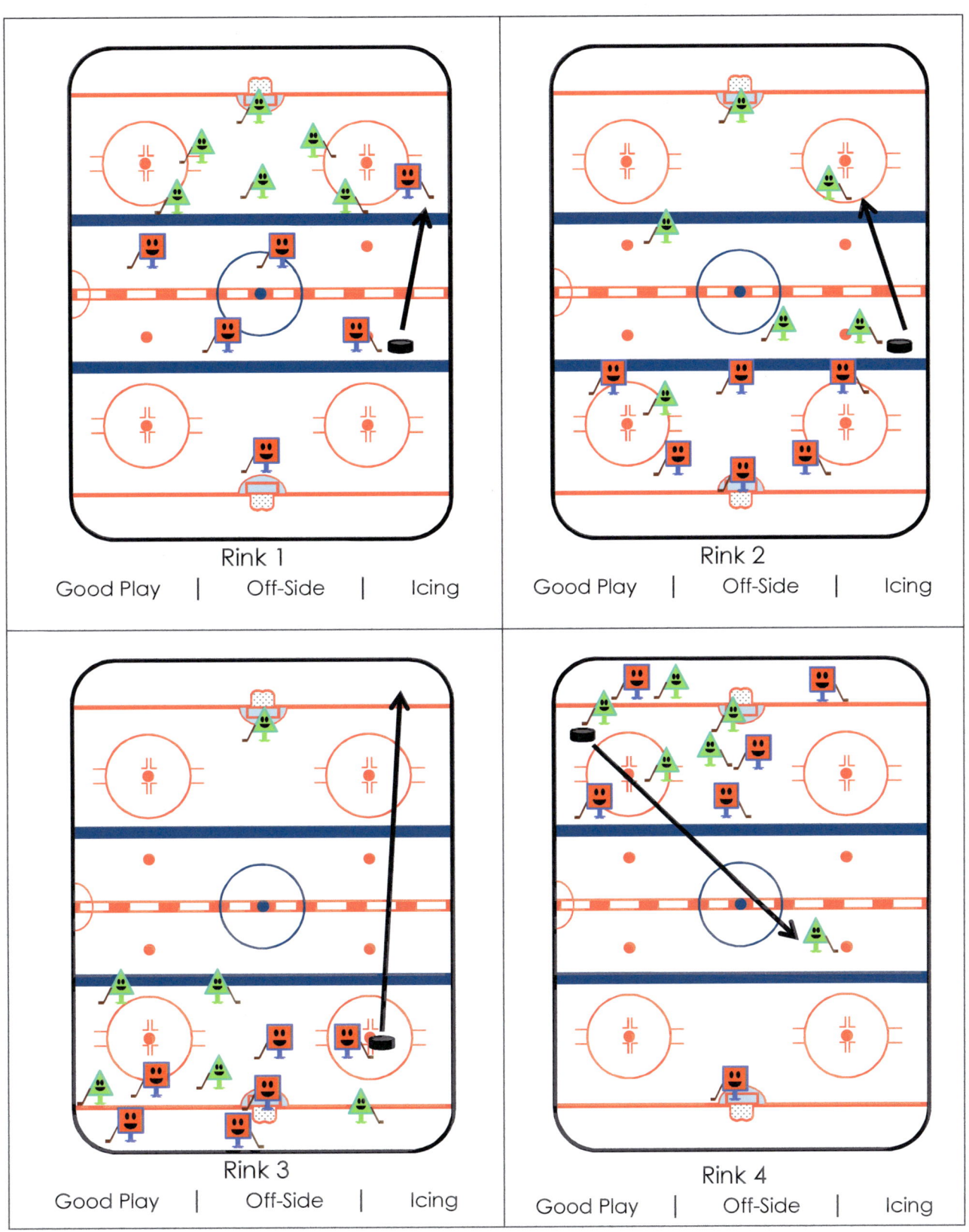

Rink 1
Good Play | Off-Side | Icing

Rink 2
Good Play | Off-Side | Icing

Rink 3
Good Play | Off-Side | Icing

Rink 4
Good Play | Off-Side | Icing

Page 53

PRACTICE: YOU MAKE THE CALL
CIRCLE the correct answer. Be careful of Off-side and Icing.

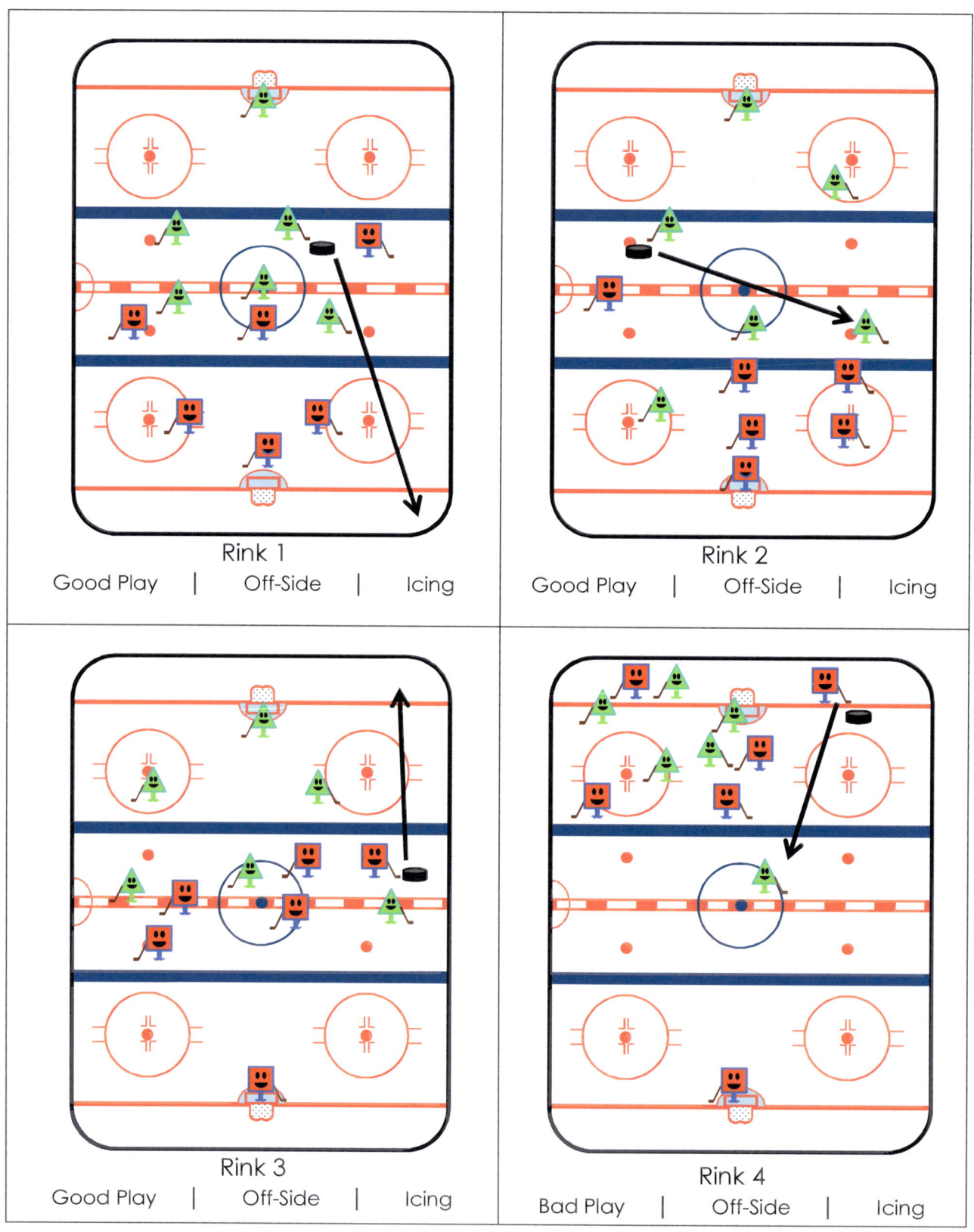

Penalties

When some other types of rules are broken the Referee may call a *PENALTY* on one or more players. Normally, the player will be sent to the *PENALTY BOX* to sit for 2 minutes. During those 2 minutes, the team who has a player in the penalty box will only be allowed to have 4 players on the ice (plus one goalie). That team is said to be playing *SHORT HANDED*. The team with more players is referred to as having a *POWER PLAY*.

Any team, no matter how many penalties they have at the same time, will be allowed to have 3 players and 1 goalie on the ice. The players who got the penalty will still have to sit in the penalty box for their penalty time.

The Red Square Team has a Power Play

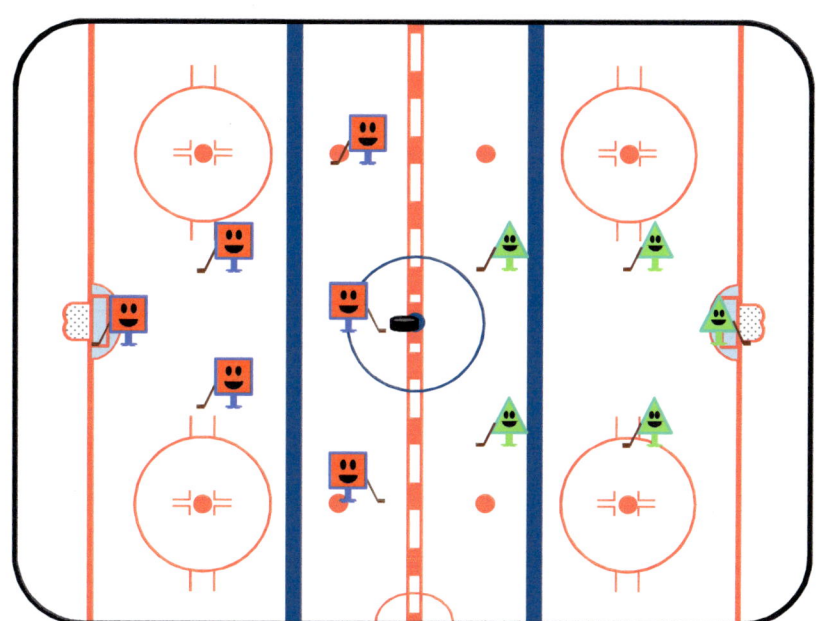

Sometimes, if a player stops another player from having a break away, then the Referee can call a *PENALTY SHOT*. During a Penalty Shot all the players clear the ice except the player who was given the penalty shot, and the opposite goalie. The player is allowed to skate from center ice with the puck, all alone, and take a shot on the other team's goalie and try to score. Only one shot is allowed. After the penalty shot, the players line up at center ice for a face-off and the game resumes.

Common Penalties

Try **NOT** to commit these types of common penalties.

CHECKING FROM BEHIND	Never, never, never push someone on their back. It is very dangerous.
CROSS CHECKING	Using the shaft of the stick, held between two hands to push another player. Use two hands on the stick when shooting, but don't use a stick to knock over other people.
HAND PASS	A hockey player cannot throw the puck. No hands allowed.
HIGH STICKING	Keep the hockey stick lower than the other player's shoulders. Helmets are for accidents. Don't hit anyone on the head.
HOOKING	When a player uses their stick to hook onto another player trying to slow them down. Don't hook your stick around someone to get a free ride.
TRIPPING	When a hockey stick is put under another players skate to trip them. Ice is already slippery enough.
SLASHING	Using the hockey stick to swing back and forth and hitting someone on the leg. It's a hockey stick, not a sword.
KICKING	Never, never, never kick another player. Skates are sharp and dangerous.
ROUGHING	No punching or pushing other players down. That's too rough.

OOPS !?!

Accidents happen, and every hockey player gets a penalty sometimes. Don't be afraid if you get a penalty. Your Coach will NOT be mad. You are NOT in trouble. After your penalty is done, go and play the game, a little safer, and everyone can keep having fun.

CONGRATULATIONS

Congratulations on completing the Hockey Basics for Kids and Beginners training book. Isn't it AMAZING how much you've learned?

Great Job! You are a hockey expert.

Earn your Certificate of Achievement

There will be a short test to show that you know how to play hockey. Find all the answers to the questions and you will have earned a Certificate of Achievement. If you get a question wrong, keep trying.

Good Luck.

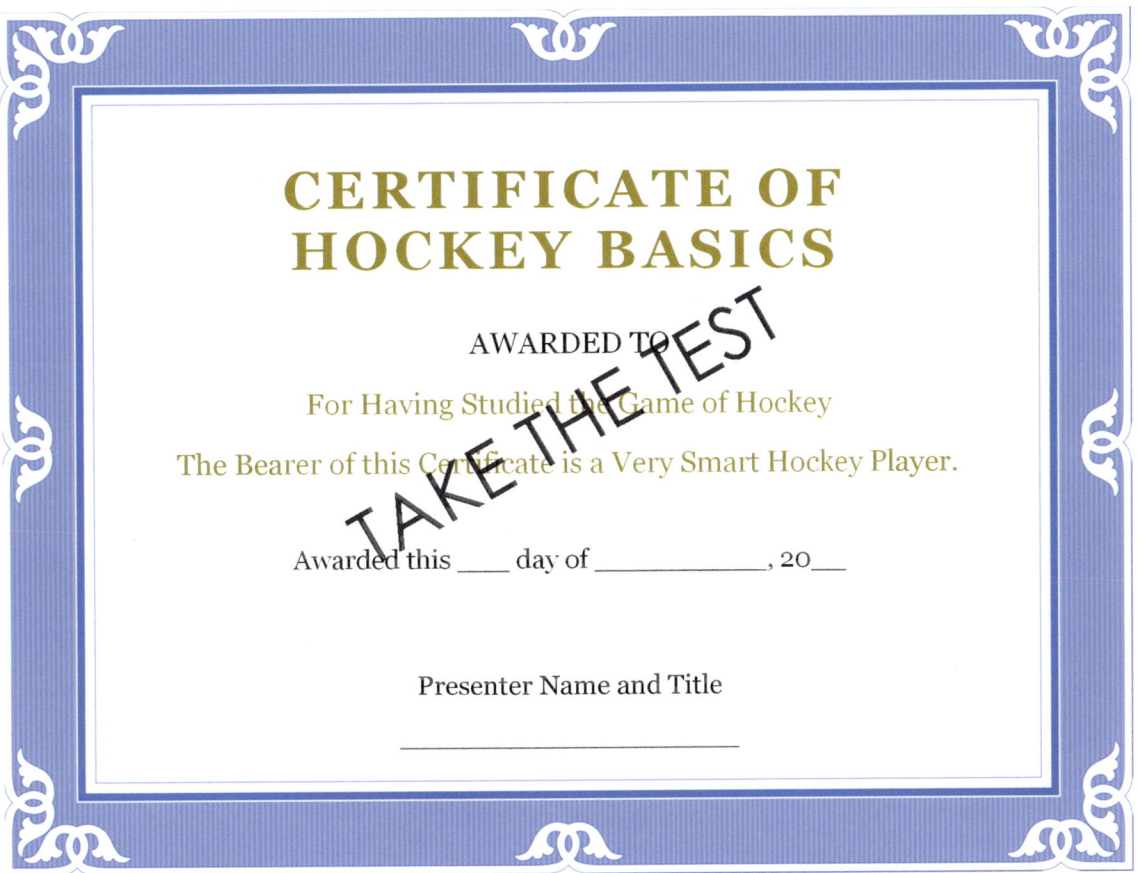

Fun Page

If you were a coach, invent a team logo that you would wear on your team shirt.

Send it to Coach John and we might put it on our website
www.HockeyCoachJohn.com
(Ask a parent)

FINAL TEST AND CERTIFICATE

Answer all the questions to earn your Hockey Basics Certificate.

CHOOSE A, B, C, or D. Write your answer in the box.

THE ICE

Question 1.
How many face-off dots does a hockey rink have?
- A. 4
- B. 5
- C. 8
- D. 9

Answer

Question 2.
The lines on the hockey rink are?
- A. 2 blue lines, 1 red line
- B. 1 goal line, 2 blue lines, 1 red line
- C. 2 red lines, 1 blue line, 2 goal lines
- D. 2 blue lines, 2 goal lines, 1 red line

Answer

Question 3.
How many cross-bars does a net have?
- A. 1
- B. 2
- C. 3

Answer

THE PEOPLE

Question 4.
Which person has the job to start and stop the clock, add goals to the score board, and write down the penalties?
- A. Coach
- B. Referee
- C. Timekeeper
- D. Assistant Coach

Answer

THE EQUIPMENT

Question 5.
Which piece of equipment protects the HEAD?
    A. Elbow Pads
    B. Helmet
    C. Socks

Answer

Question 6.
Which piece of equipment protects the LEGS?
    A. Gloves
    B. Cup
    C. Shin Guards

Answer

Question 7.
Which piece of equipment protects the ARMS?
    A. Suspenders
    B. Neck Guard
    C. Elbow Pads

Answer

Question 8.
When should a player put on their ice skates?
    A. BEFORE they put on their hockey pants.
    B. AFTER they put on their hockey pants.

Answer

Question 9.
The puck keeps sliding off your stick. You buy some tape to put on your stick. Where should you put the tape on?
    A. Shaft
    B. Blade
    C. Shin Guard

Answer

PLAYERS AND POSITIONS

Question 10.

What player is responsible for guarding the net?
- A. Forwards
- B. Left Defense
- C. Goalie

Answer

Question 11.

Which area of the ice should the Right Defense play in?
Hint:
- B, D, and C are FORWARDS
- E and A are DEFENSE

Answer

Question 12.

Which area of the ice should the Left Wing play in?
Hint:
- B, D, and C are FORWARDS
- E and A are DEFENSE

Answer

THE GAME

Question 13.
How many periods are there in a hockey game?
  A. 1
  B. 2
  C. 3
  D. 4

Answer

Question 14.
A player got the puck and skated all the way down the ice, all alone. What did the player get?
  A. Rebound
  B. Face-off
  C. Break away

Answer

Question 15.
One team is very happy because they won the game, and one team is sad because they lost the game. At the end of the game, what should both teams do at center ice?
  A. Do a team dance
  B. Talk about who is the best team
  C. Shake hands and say "Good Game".

Answer

ZONES

Question 16.
What zone is the middle part of the ice is called?
  A. Defensive zone
  B. Offensive zone
  C. Neutral zone

Answer

Question 17.
The Goalie always stays in the Defensive Zone?
  A. True
  B. False

Answer

RULES

Question 18.

The Referee might blow the whistle when:
- A. The Goalie covers the puck
- B. A player is off-sides
- C. There is an icing play
- D. A player commits a penalty
- E. A, B, C, and D are correct.

Answer

Question 19.

When a player crosses the offensive blue line before the puck crosses the blue line, the Referee will stop the game because of what?
- A. Cherry-picking
- B. Icing
- C. Off-sides
- D. Hat Trick

Answer

BONUS

Question 20.

Is ice hockey fun to play?
- A. Yes
- B. For Sure
- C. True
- D. I Love Hockey

Answer

Fun Page

Your team has WON. Draw a picture of the trophy.

Send it to Coach John and we might put it on our website
www.HockeyCoachJohn.com
(Ask a parent)

Answer Pages

Practice: Help the Players (Page 3)
  Rink 1: Red team top bench.
  Rink 2: Red team top bench.
  Rink 3: Red team top bench (notice red team penalty box)
  Rink 4: Green team top bench (notice green penalty box)

Practice: Color the Lines (Page 5)
  Color 2 RED goal lines, 2 BLUE lines, 1 RED line.

Practice: Find the Lines (Page 5)
  Rink 7 is the only correct rink.

Practice: Circles and Dots (Page 7)
  Color 4 RED circles, 1 BLUE circle, 8 RED dots, 1 BLUE dot.

Practice: Missing Pieces (Page 10)
  Rink 1: 4 red circles (plus hash marks), and 1 blue circle.
  Rink 2: 8 red dots, 1 blue dot.
  Rink 3: 2 goal lines, 2 blue lines, and 6 sets of hash marks.
  Rink 4: 2 nets, 1 red line.

Practice: The Layout of the Ice - Word Find
  See picture to the right. (Page 11)

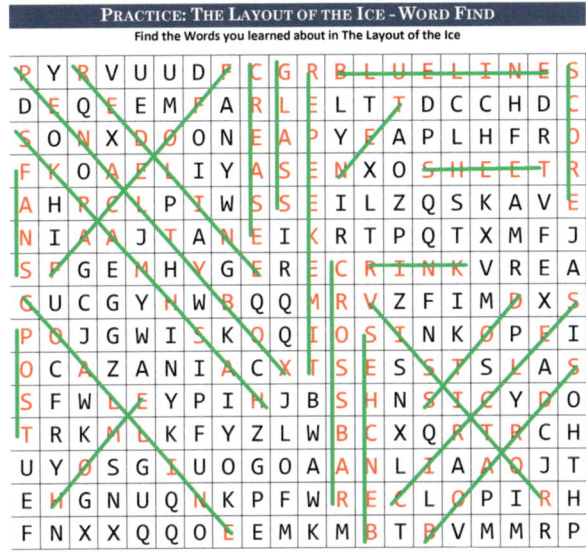

Practice: Draw an Ice Hockey Rink (Page 12)
  See example of Ice Hockey Rink in this book.

Practice: Dress the Player (Page 19)
  See equipment list in this book.

Practice: Connect the Picture to the Word (Pg 23)
  Go to: www.HockeyCoachJohn.com

Practice: Protective Equipment Crossword
  See picture to the right. (Page 24)

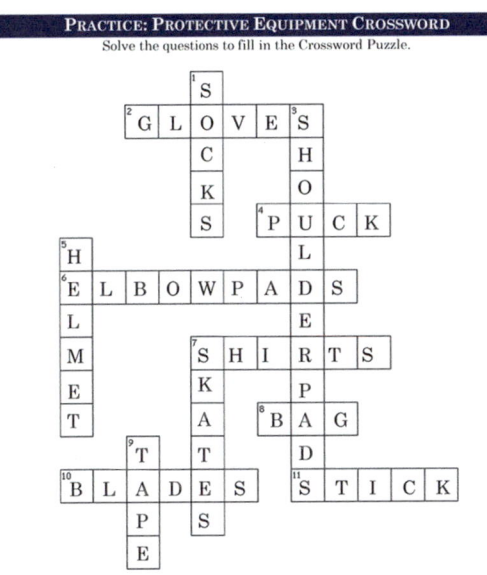

Practice: Forwards and Positions (Page 32)
 Rink 1: RW   **Rink 2**: C, RW   **Rink 3**: LW
 Rink 4: LW, RW   **Rink 5**: C   **Rink 6**: LW, C

Practice: Who is Not in the Correct Position (Page 33, 34)
 Rink 1: C   **Rink 2**: LW   **Rink 3**: LD, RD   **Rink 4**: LW, C, RW
 Rink 5: LD, LW   **Rink 6**: C, RW, LD   **Rink 7**: LW, RW   **Rink 8**: LW, C, RW

Practice: Start The Game (Page 37)
 Go to: www.HockeyCoachJohn.com

Practice: Break Away Maze (Page 39)
 See picture to the right.

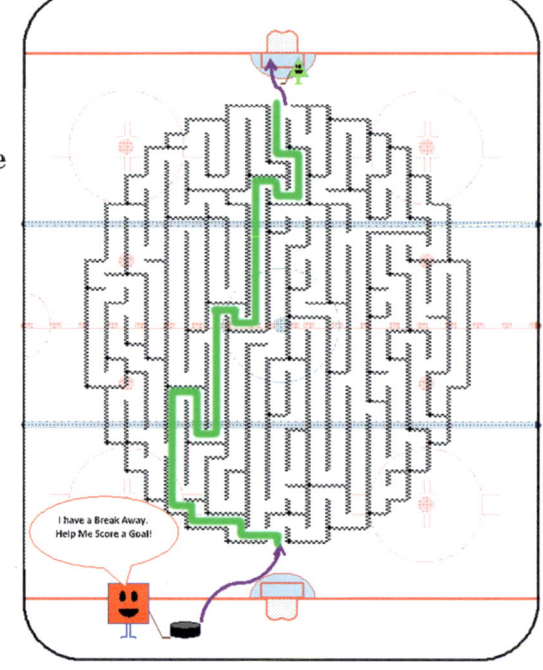

Practice: Word Find with Mystery Code (Page 43)
 Mystery Code: HOCKEY IS FUN TO PLAY

Practice: Know the Zones / Stay in the Correct Zone (Page 48, 49)
 Rink 1: ▲ Neutral ■ Defensive
 Rink 2: ▲ Offensive ■ Defensive
 Rink 3: ▲ Defensive ■ Offensive
 Rink 4: ▲ Offensive ■ Defensive
 Rink 5: ▲ Neutral ■ Neutral
 Rink 6: ▲ Defensive ■ Offensive
 Rink 7: ▲ Neutral ■ Defensive

Practice: You Make the Call (Page 53)
 Rink 1: Off-side.   **Rink 2**: Good Play.
 Rink 3: Icing.   **Rink 4**: Good Play.

Practice: You Make the Call (Page 54)
 Rink 1: Icing.   **Rink 2**: Good Play.   **Rink 3**: Good Play.   **Rink 4**: Bad Play.

FINAL TEST (Page 59 - 63)

Question 1	D	Question 11	A
Question 2	D	Question 12	B
Question 3	A	Question 13	C
Question 4	C	Question 14	C
Question 5	B	Question 15	C
Question 6	C	Question 16	C
Question 7	C	Question 17	A
Question 8	B	Question 18	E
Question 9	B	Question 19	C
Question 10	C	**Bonus Q 20**	ABCD

Index of Words Learned

A
ASSISTANT COACHES, 13

B
BAG, 16
BENCHES, 2
BLADE, 22
BLADES, 17
BLUE LINE, 4
BOARDS, 2
BREAK AWAY, 38
BUTT-END, 22

C
CENTER, 29
CENTER ICE, 6
CHERRY PICKER, 31
CIRCLES, 6
COACH, 13
CREASE, 8
CROSSBAR, 8
CUP, 16

D
DEFENSE PLAYERS, 13
DEFENSIVE ZONE, 45
DOTS, 6

E
ELBOW PADS, 17
END ZONES, 44
EQUIPMENT, 15

F
FACE-OFF, 6
FANS, 2
FORWARD PLAYERS, 13
FORWARDS, 29

G
GARTER BELT, 16
GLASS, 2
GLOVES, 17
GOAL LINE, 4
GOAL POST, 8
GOALIE, 26
GOALIES, 13
GOOD GAME, 42

H
HASH MARKS, 6
HAT TRICK, 38
HEAD COACH, 13
HELMET, 17
HOME, 2

I
ICING, 51
ICING THE PUCK, 51

J
JERSEY, 20

K
KNOB, 22

L
LEFT DEFENSE, 27
LEFT HANDED, 21
LEFT WING, 29
LH. See LEFT HANDED
LINESMAN, 51

N
NECK GUARD, 17
NET, 8
NETS, 8
NETTING, 8
NEURTAL ZONE, 45
NEUTRAL ZONE, 44

O
OFFENSE, 29
OFFENSIVE ZONE, 45
OFFSIDE, 52
OFF-SIDE, 52
OVERTIME, 42

P
PANTS, 16
PASS, 38
PENALTY, 55
PENALTY BOX, 2, 55
PENALTY SHOT, 55
PERIODS, 40
POINT, 38
POSITION, 13
POST, 8
POWER PLAY, 55
PUCK, 20

R
REBOUND, 38
RED LINE, 4
REFEREE, 13
REFEREE CREASE, 6
RH. See RIGHT HANDED
RIGHT DEFENSE, 27
RIGHT HANDED, 21
RIGHT WING, 29
RINK, 2

S
SAVING, 26
SCORE, 38
SCORE BOARD, 40
SCORED, 38
SCORED A GOAL, 38
SHAFT, 22
SHEET, 2
SHIN GUARDS, 16
SHIRT, 17, 20
SHIRTS, 20
SHOOT, 38
SHORT HANDED, 55
SHOULDER PADS, 16
SHUT OUT, 38
SKATE BLADES, 16
SKATES, 16
SOCKS, 16
STICK, 21
STICK HANDLING, 22
SUSPENDERS, 17

T
TAPE, 22
TEAM, 13
TIE GAME, 41
TIME KEEPER, 2, 13

V
VERSUS, 41
VISITOR, 2

W
WHISTLE, 13
WIN THE GAME, 42

Z
ZONES, 44

Made in United States
Troutdale, OR
10/03/2025